The Morning After Death

The republication of this book
has been made possible
due to the generous assistance
of the Board of Trustees
of Furman University

The Morning After Death

L. D. Johnson

Smyth & Helwys Publishing, Inc.®
Macon, Georgia

ISBN 1-57312-029-4
The Morning After Death
L. D. Johnson

Copyright © 1995
Smyth & Helwys Publishing, Inc.®
6316 Peake Road
Macon, Georgia
31210-3960
1-800-747-3016

Library of Congress Cataloging-in-Publication Data
Johnson, L. D., 1916–
   The morning after death / L. D. Johnson.
   xiv + 156   5" x 7½"
   Originally published: Nashville Broadman Press,
   © 1978.
   ISBN 1-57312-029-4   (alk. paper)
   1. Johnson, Carole, 1939–1962. 2. Baptists—United
   States—Biography. 3. Grief. 4. Theodicy. I. Title.
   BX6495.J49J63   1995
   242'.4—dc20   95-8572
                                              CIP

This book is lovingly dedicated to

Elaine Johnson Yeatts
and
Claud Roland Johnson,

who in Carole's death lost not only
a sister but a close friend.

L. D. Johnson

For his service to Furman University as Chaplain for
almost fifteen years;

For his inspiring and provocative teaching in the
Department of Religion;

For the organization and direction of the Furman
University pastors School, the largest one-week
program of continuing theological education
in the nation;

For his profound and inspiring sermons at Furman;

For his sincere and caring service as pastor and
counselor to Furman' students, faculty, and other
personnel;

For his scholarly and stimulating authorship of books
and articles;

For the nationwide recognition he acquired as preacher
and lecturer;

The Board of Trustees of Furman University expresses
profound gratitude and affection for L. D. Johnson,
his wife, Marion, and their children.

Thomas S. Hartness   *David E. Shi*
Chair, Board of Trustees   President

October 11, 1994

Contents

Foreword

I am highly pleased that this book by L. D. Johnson is being published. It is a distinctly Christian response to the overwhelming amount of material being published today on death and dying. *The Morning After Death* provides a needed antibiotic for the spirit against the hazy spiritualism, wizardry, and necromancy that pervade much current thinking about death and dying. I read the manuscript three times; and each time I felt a fresh flow of spiritual energy from the living, human documentary of a pastor's wrestling with God through traumatic grief, of a young girl's pilgrimage from birth to maturity in a pastor's home, of a struggling prophet's effort to speak through his own experience to other struggling prophets, and of a disciplined craftsman in the care and cure of souls offering real oases of strength for facing life and death.

The Morning After Death is more than a story of the death of one of the family, an exquisite daughter, Carole, snatched from the family by an automobile crash. It is the story of a whole family, much of it coming out of Carole's own writings. In both prose and poetry she left the essence of an autobiography of the private life of a "preacher's kid." In this book Carole, though dead, yet speaks a straight-on word about the bond of humor, irony, tragedy, and celebration that is the life of most pastors and their families. While introducing us to Carole, her father, without consciously intending to do so, has given us the most candid account of the inner life of a working pastor's family that I have ever read.

This book also reveals the true church; it vivifies the church's corporate fellowship as it illuminates the presence of Christ in the most unassuming and natural ways. The churches and Christians around L. D. Johnson did not make long speeches to him. Instead, they braved inclement weather to help recover the shattered body of his daughter. They sat where he sat. They affirmed the negative feelings of a man in grief. They expressed their beliefs in a God who could respond to anger, frustration, and grief. The book offers fresh appreciation for the positive strengths of the church.

The last three chapters dare to grapple with love and evil, the "whereness" of the dead, and the affirmations of the Christian preacher in the face of his personal experience with death. There are no pious assurances in the maudlin greeting-card style. There are no neat "proofs" of the resurrection that sound better on Easter than on the day of death's awful hush. Instead, this book meets head-on the issue of whether we live in a trustworthy though mysterious world when we must walk through the valley of bereavement. It affirms the resurrection of the dead by the God of the living without avoiding the simplicity of our ignorance and the necessity of the serene faith that God can be trusted. This is a book to read and share with others.

WAYNE E. OATES

Preface

The Morning After Death was written at the University of Exeter, England. Carole, our firstborn, had been a student there. She came home for her senior year at Westhampton College, University of Richmond, and then went away again to earn a master's degree at the University of North Carolina. In her first year as a high school teacher of English in Richmond, Virginia, Carole was killed in an automobile accident while traveling home to Greenville, South Carolina, for Christmas on December 21, 1962, the day after her twenty-third birthday.

As grief waned, I began to think about writing something on the meaning of Carole's life and death. However, every time I got close to the project, our irretrievable loss loomed too painful and private to expect any save the narrowing circle of her friends and ours to find it worth reading. Years lapsed. The need persisted. Finally I asked for a brief sabbatical from my post as chaplain and professor of religion at Furman University to go to Exeter, a place where Carole found intellectual and esthetic stimulation. Her weekly letters home the year she was there were a guidebook not only to what had intrigued and inspired her but also to the intricacies of her self.

Thus Exeter became a pilgrimage for my wife, Marion, and

me. We were there in spring, and Devon and Cornwall had put on their Sunday best. Manicured hedgerows lined rolling green meadows where sheep and cattle grazed. Rich russet-colored plowed fields offered warm contrast to lush green blankets spread over the earth. From backyard patches to spacious grounds of grand estates, gardens were in stunning profusion of primroses, daffodils, anemones, tulips, camellias, azaleas, red and white rhododendron, and dozens of other less familiar flowering plants and trees. The gorse on Dartmoor streaked that bleak expanse with brilliant gold. The earth teemed with life. We understood what had captured our daughter's imagination.

At Exeter we met people who remembered Carole, even after sixteen years. Mr. and Mrs. William Jackson, once resident managers of "Monty," the university house in which she lived, spoke affectionately and offered us their kindness. Miss Rosemary Barber and Miss Barbara Rhead, students with Carole the year she was at Exeter, befriended us and enlarged our knowledge of that year at the university. Mrs. Valery Scott, Carole's roommate at Exeter, talked with us at length by long distance. We met Carole's two teachers, Mr. Keith Salter and Dr. A. N. Parkinson, both of whom had expanded her love of English literature. The extraordinary kindness of people we chanced to meet and came to know as friends, notably Mrs. John Caldwell, the Honorable Grace Lambert, and Mr. and Mrs. Francis Sleeman, belies the provincial American notion of British aloofness. Nowhere could I have found a more congenial environment for reflection and writing. I am grateful to Furman and Provost Francis W. Bonner for releasing me.

Marion was of invaluable assistance, allowing me to write while she did chores, encouraging me to persevere, and reliving with me the bittersweet memories of Carole's life and death. Our other children, Mrs. Elaine Yeatts and the Reverend C.

Roland Johnson, supported us and helped remember our family record. They are no less dear to us. The loss of one child does not diminish love for one's other children, any more than one's other children diminish grief for the loss of one child.

I am indebted to my colleague, Mrs. Eugenia Cantrell, who for many years has deciphered my ragged manuscripts with skill and good humor. I appreciate my other colleague in chaplaincy, Dr. James M. Pitts, for presiding over our multiple-ring "circus" in my absence. I owe a special debt to another Furman colleague, Mrs. Maryneal Jones, for her tireless effort to make what I have written more readable.

To all who grieved for Carole and to all who sorrowed because they know us, we give thanks for caring. Hundreds of such friends have helped create a Carole M. Johnson Memorial Scholarship Fund which now from its income provides two handsome annual college scholarships for women.

If people who read this account are reminded of the beauty and wonder inherent in our humanity and find added courage to resist the selfishness and terrifying brutality of our at-the-edge-of-darkness age, I shall be gratified. If it helps someone to be honest in his own grief, not cramming his doubt and anger and remorse into a locked box, I shall feel the more rewarded. But mainly I needed to write what I have written.

L. D. JOHNSON

1.
The Morning After Death

Dying! To be afraid of thee
One must to thine Artillery
Have left exposed a Friend.

Emily Dickinson

The day Carole was killed had an uneasy quality about it. We awakened to leaden skies and chill more penetrating than brisk-cold. There were suggestions we might have a white Christmas. Marion didn't like it; neither did I. Carole would be leaving Richmond, Virginia, at one o'clock, after classes were dismissed from Hermitage High School where she was in her first year as an English teacher. She would be driving home—four hundred miles to Greenville, South Carolina.

Before breakfast we talked about the weather and decided to call Carole and tell her to come on the train or bus, or to fly. I was rushing to my study at First Baptist Church, Greenville, where I had been pastor only a few months. The day would be busy. It was Friday. Sunday morning's sermon was not yet in preachable condition. It was Marion who called Carole to say the weather down our way looked threatening, and we wished she would stay off the highway. What else could you say to a twenty-three-year-old daughter who had been grown-up almost all her life, who had hitchhiked over Europe, and was a high-school teacher in a distant city?

I didn't talk to her and that has been part of my anguish. "Oh, Mama, you worry too much," she had said. "I'll be all right. You

15

know I won't take chances." I could have said nothing her mother did not say, but perhaps she would have listened to me because she knew I am less cautious than Marion. But I didn't talk to her, and I shall never stop regretting it.

I went to the church and began pulling the Christmas sermon together. Familiar themes, about which I have heard or preached a thousand sermons, are the hardest. How can one improve on the biblical original?

One of my errands that Friday was a trip to the bank for new money to put in Christmas envelopes for Marion and the children. For many years at our house this little ritual has been recognized as the annual visitation of "Scrooge." Scrooge doesn't hurt himself, it being understood that Scrooge-money is to buy something needed like clothes or to be put in savings. Nobody squanders Scrooge money at our house. About eleven o'clock I went to the bank. There was a biting sharpness to the air. Somebody in the bank had heard that roads across North Carolina were icy. An alarm went off in my mind. I resolved to call Carole at once, for she had to come that way.

Going back to the office, I turned into a camera shop to get film for the holidays. Some friends from the congregation were there, and we stood around and talked a few minutes. Even so, I thought there was ample time to reach Carole before she left school. There wasn't. Because the weather in Richmond warned snow, classes had been dismissed an hour early.

When I called, the secretary answering said, "I think she's just left, but wait, I'll go see." I had missed her by only a few minutes. Growing foreboding took hold of my insides.

Several times I called Carole's apartment. No answer. She had left directly from school. We had all made that trip time and time again. There is nothing to it. Don't be jumpy. Nothing is going to happen, I told myself.

Since it was four days before Christmas, all the people who worked with me at the church left early. I was still wrestling with the Sunday morning text. There was a switch beside my desk to shut off the ringing of the telephone when I was studying, writing, or counseling. That afternoon I forgot to activate the bell on my telephone, so I was sitting at the desk oblivious to news that would affect every day of the rest of our lives.

Near Oxford, North Carolina, a tractor-trailer collided with Carole's little compact and collapsed it into junk. She died in minutes. Somebody told me later the only thing she said was, "It hurts so much." (It still does, Carole, after all these years.)

The mortuary in Oxford tried repeatedly to get me at home, refusing to leave a message. Though she did not know the source of the call, the urgent tones filled Marion with grave apprehension. She telephoned one of the church staff to find me. My close friend and associate in the ministry, the Rev. Herbert Sargent, brought me the number to call. I dialed. The instant I heard the word "mortuary" my body stiffened as if electrically shocked. The man asked if Carole Marion Johnson was my daughter. I could only stammer, "Yes." And then he told me she had been killed in a wreck near his town. I do not know if he said anything else. I think I hung up on him, too stunned to ask questions. I remember dropping the receiver on the hook and staring at my friend and saying, "My God, Herb, Carole's been killed!"

Herbert went home with me in my car. For some inexplicable reason I insisted on driving—an irrational thing—but it seemed important to me at the time. I can remember only that my repeated moans, "Oh, my Baby, my poor Baby," were punctuated by Herbert's pleas for me to be careful.

Marion and our other two children, Elaine, at the time a junior at Westhampton College, and Roland, then a tenth grader, instinctively knew that we had been enveloped in tragedy. For more than an hour, while I was closeted in the study, they had been frantic. When I pulled into the driveway, they were waiting at the back door. I could only cry out, "Carole has been killed in a wreck! Carole is dead!"

Bad news travels fast. Quickly our house filled with friends and parishioners. In stunned brokenness our family tried to cope with death's intrusion. Reenacting one of the race's oldest rituals, we clung to each other and wept.

The next morning three Danville, Virginia, men who had known Carole from her infancy set out under hazardous driving conditions to do the most loving thing they knew to do for Carole and her family. They manned the hearse that brought her body to Greenville.

We had lived in Greenville only a short time, having come to the church after a three-year stay at the University of Richmond. Though they had known us so briefly, and Carole hardly at all, the congregation surrounded us with care. People did what they could. It is not possible to catalog the separate and corporate expressions of concern. They grieved with us and for us.

The church paid the expenses of Carole's funeral without telling us it was done. We reimbursed the church but the act touched us deeply, and still does. One kindness I remember for its simple beauty. A colleague came and stayed without offering condolence speeches, diverting attention from our sorrow, or taking over things we needed to do. He did not try to make decisions for us, shield us from people we wanted to see, or ask us to see people we did not wish to see. Nearby if needed, out of sight if not, he was just there. That was genuine and important ministry to a grieving family.

Carole's funeral was held in the Greenville church, and we buried her in Danville, Virginia, beside her little brother,

Richard, who had died in 1958 at four-and-a-half. His death had hurt us, too, but he had been born with a severely defective heart and never had an even chance to grow up. Perhaps some believe that one person's death is the same as another's, but I do not. To be sure, "any man's death diminishes me," but Carole's devastated me. For reasons which elude my understanding she was a most uncommon person in my eyes.

At her burial my friend, Howard Lee, read 1 Corinthians 13 and offered a prayer of thanksgiving for Carole's life. Again, friends and former parishioners of First Baptist Church, Danville, surrounded us with love. We came back home and took up our work. What else could be done? What had God called us to be, if not faithful?

A few days later I received a letter from a man in Reidsville, North Carolina, saying that he had heard of our grief. He enclosed a sermon I had sent him many years before. At some point during my seventeen years as pastor of the First Baptist Church in Danville, I had preached about "How Christ Helps Us with the Problem of Death." This man had asked for a copy. He said in his letter that the sermon had comforted him, and perhaps I needed to remind myself of what I had said.

Do I believe what I said about Christ and death in that sermon? I asked myself from the bottom of the pit. I do. The Sunday following Carole's burial I went into the pulpit and delivered the sermon as best I could. It is now sixteen years later. I still stand by that sermon. Hundreds of copies of it have been given to people who have experienced grief or who have been concerned about friends in grief. We put it in a rack in the student center of our college, and the rack empties in a few days. This is not because it is a great literary achievement but because it speaks to the universal hurt. I cannot write what I do not mean about death. There is much I do not understand, but I am sure that in Christ I have found comfort and hope. Because I believe what that sermon says, I decided to include it at the end of this book as a part of this witness to Carole.

Set beside the monstrous evils of war, mass starvation, and pestilence, the death of one bright and beautiful girl on a highway seems insignificant. The soil is perpetually reddened with human blood. Why should one girl's fatal accident lay claim to anyone's already overtaxed capacity for sorrow? There is no reason at all except that her story is the one I know as her father, and her death raises the ageless questions about meaning with which sooner or later everyone must deal.

Of course, she was an extraordinary person to us. We grieve for her because she was young and in love and eager for life— not old and fulfilled and ready to give up physical existence. But this is not to suggest that her death was more painful than the death of someone else's loved one, or the loss of her greater. Rather, I want to be able to gather up some of the sighs, hurts, hopes, and affirmations common to all of us who have lost vital and precious love incarnate in a life too soon ended.

Here is not simply the story of a beautiful girl who died just as she was beginning to fulfill the considerable promise people saw in her but also a chronicle of her father's long struggle with the issues of human existence. What meaning can be assigned to life apart from consideration of death? To ignore death is to ignore the ultimate question of life's purpose. For a long time I have sensed that life and death are indivisible aspects of the same reality—namely, existence. But since Carole's death it has seemed imperative that I name the place where meaning is enveloped in mystery and that I embrace both meaning and mystery by faith.

The most important resource, other than memory, for this book has been Carole's papers and letters. She had a voracious appetite for knowledge and an uncommon gift for translating beauty of the mind and heart into vivid and lucid language. Her letters were mostly filled with the exuberance of a blithe spirit leaping through extravagantly beautiful spaces. Occasionally, as will be faithfully documented, she was sad, depressed, doubting, angry. She was one of the most fully alive persons I have known. And that is why her death seems to me incongruous.

She was an Emily Dickinson fan, and I learned from our other daughter, Elaine, that Carole's favorite poem was the one which says:

> The Bustle in a House
> The Morning after Death
> Is solemnest of industries
> Enacted upon Earth—
>
> The Sweeping up the Heart
> And putting Love away
> We shall not want to use again
> Until Eternity.[1]

Immediately after her death, we did put her things away in the attic. There was no problem about material things. She did not have many. Things held little fascination for her. But she had many books and had kept her own compositions—term papers, exams, journals, and numerous speeches spanning high school and college. They were from a variety of circumstances such as church services, college chapels, and speech contests. Odds and ends of paper contained rhymed thoughts, some of which are included here. On other sheets she had copied bits of verse. Among these were Byron's lovely lines:

> There is a pleasure in the pathless woods,
> There is a rapture on the lonely shore,
> There is society where none intrudes
> By the deep sea, and music in its roar.[2]

Another was the familiar sonnet of Elizabeth Barrett Browning to her husband, Robert, "How Do I Love Thee?" These were not casual or coincidental collections. They were among her cherished belongings because they described her own heart—her sense of closeness to the natural world, her faith in God, and her considerable capacity for human love.

She had copied some lines from Tennyson's profound affirmation, "In Memoriam":

> Strong Son of God, immortal Love,
>   Whom we, that have not seen thy face,
>   By faith, and faith alone, embrace,
> Believing where we cannot prove;
>
> . . . .
>
> We have but faith: we cannot know,
>   For knowledge is of things we see;
>   And yet we trust it comes from thee,
> A beam in darkness: let it grow.
>
> Let knowledge grow from more to more,
>   For knowledge is of things we see;
>   And yet we trust it comes from thee,
> A beam in darkness: let it grow.
>
> Let knowledge grow from more to more,
>   But more of reverence in us dwell;
>   That mind and soul, according well,
> May make one music as before.[3]

Written following the sudden death of his Cambridge friend, Arthur Hallam, the poem expresses Tennyson's resolution of the inner conflict between belief in God's goodness and the mysterious and senseless loss of one of God's best and most useful creations. Among Carole's papers I found comments about the Tennyson statement of faith. She had written: "It took Tennyson seventeen years of wrestling with himself to make him conclude that the only answer was to believe by faith in a God of love."

I do not know at what stage of her intellectual and spiritual development she made the observation about Tennyson, but like many other things written in her small, carefully-formed script, the words have an awesome prescience about her own abbreviated life. After these years of wrestling with the question of the meaning of her death I find myself no further along than Tennyson was about Hallam's. I trust, but I do not understand.

Whatever she wrote had the distinctive mark of her own warm, vivid self, and reflected moods ranging from elation to wonder to depression to annoyance to appreciation. She left a considerable legacy, not because she lived long but because she lived with her eyes open and took time to record what her heart and mind felt. Because we could not bear further pain at that point we swept up our hearts and put love away. But the time came to get it out and put together a chronicle of Carole's short life.

2.
In the Beginning

A simple child that lightly draws its breath
And feels its life in every limb,
What should it know of death?
William Wordsworth, "We Are Seven"

Carole's name was related to the coincidence of her birth five days before Christmas. She was our "Christmas Carol-e," the *e* added because we liked it. Large delft-blue eyes with long lashes were part of her original equipment. When we brought her home from the hospital I was both proud and embarrassed. I had never handled a baby, and this one was tiny and looked like a fragile doll with red, peeling skin.

We were seminarians living below the poverty level in late Depression times, but we were too busy and happy to know or care. In spring I mowed lawns and in fall raked leaves for thirty cents an hour. Later I became an entrepreneur, selling women's shoes on weekends and holidays, sometimes making eight or ten dollars on good days before Easter and Christmas. Twice a year I enjoyed a bonanza, replacing the warning lights atop the seminary smokestack. For ascending the iron-rung ladder inside that hundred-foot chimney, hanging over the rim, and installing four light bulbs, I earned grocery money for a week—$5.00! When I became a doctoral candidate the pay went up to $7.50 a trip.

The first winter and spring of Carole's life we bundled her up every weekend to drive in our secondhand car to one or the other of our rural churches. Those were daylight-to-midnight marathons. At first Marion put Carole in her bassinet and stood guard to keep those country women, most of whom had raised a house full of children, from picking her up. They soon persuaded us that a baby isn't worth having unless you can bounce it on your lap, pass it around for everybody to have a turn, and feed it table scraps. Those women loved Carole and taught us to relax with her. On a Sunday afternoon when she was twelve months old she took her first steps, toddling across the room in one of those country houses. Strange how well I remember that day and place.

When Carole was nearly three, Elaine was born. Always the efficient, no-nonsense type, Elaine arrived almost before Marion could convince the nurses in the ward that the baby was coming. Thus began a relationship that had all the elements of love, admiration, rivalry, hostility, and ultimate close companionship familiar to sisters. At one stage older sister found younger sister quite difficult (truthfully, they couldn't stand each other). When they were about thirteen and ten, respectively, things got tense from time to time, and this went on for about five years. Elaine wanted to sleep in Carole's room, wear her clothes, hang around when she was with her friends—the whole universal drama of older-younger sister rivalry.

Elaine now has two little girls of her own. The difference in their ages is almost the same as the age difference between Elaine and Carole. The interplay of the timeless dynamic of fierce love-dislike, affirmation-rejection at work in the lives of these little girls is fascinating to observe. Watching them together is like seeing an old movie. When Elaine emerged from Carole's shadow and began to experience her own selfhood, the two became fast and mutually admiring interdependents. After Carole's death Elaine said with simple eloquence: "I've lost not only my sister but also my best friend."

By the time Elaine was born, World War II was blazing and many of my fellow graduates in ministry had accepted commissions as chaplains. While we were trying to decide what to do, a call came for me to become pastor of First Baptist Church, Danville. I had never heard of Danville, Virginia. It was even. They had never heard of me, so we took each other quite on faith, which has about it a certain biblical merit; and it turned out to be a pivotal decision. Seventeen years later—lacking four months (January, 1943, until September, 1959) —we were still in Danville.

When we arrived, Carole was barely three, a petite, vivacious child with compelling eyes. Perhaps it was because she was the oldest, or maybe it is only that I have unwittingly surrounded her with an aura of maturity beyond her years, that I remember her childhood as uncomplicated and pleasant. There were stressful times, of course. When she was four or five she had scarlet fever and developed pneumonia, which gave us a scare because the miracle drugs were largely unknown then. When she was about eight she broke her arm roller-skating. Marion remembers that day, for she was entertaining ladies at tea when Carole came in holding her arm and crying. Never imagining that it was broken, Marion took her upstairs, propped her arm on a pillow and told her it would feel better in a while, then went back and finished her tea. Typically, Carole remained upstairs in silence, nursing a broken arm.

When Carole and Elaine were seven and four, our son, Roland, was born. Soon we realized he was having difficulty breathing, and it was determined he had a congenital heart defect, an extra load he carries with good spirit and gutty determination. He, too, has his own family now, with two healthy little boys. His indomitable will to live up to and beyond the limits imposed by a heart that wasn't put together right and his rejection of self-pity or the temptation to trade on his handicap are an inspiration.

One summer before Carole was ten we were staying at a summer camp out in the boondocks in Maryland, where I was "camp preacher" for a week. The family had come along for an inexpensive vacation, the kind preachers' families become accustomed to. On a Saturday afternoon Carole was running down a hill when she tripped and fell on a broken soft drink bottle, slashing her right leg open almost from knee to ankle. I picked her up and carried her to the car to drive fifteen miles to Annapolis, trying meanwhile to soothe her cries of fear and pain. The intern on duty did the best he could, but to her grave she bore a broad scar down the front of her leg.

When she was about twelve, Elaine nine, and Roland four or five, we drove to California. There were no interstate highways, and air conditioning in a car was an unheard-of luxury. We were crowded, and it was hot. In Fresno, California, Carole came down with a sore throat and fever. This was before polio vaccine and, of course, we imagined the worst. The doctor who saw her took a wait-and-see attitude, which did not relieve our apprehension. Carole later told us that she overheard us making the decision to have her sleep alone because of possible contagion. That was a bad night, not only for us, but unnecessarily for her as well.

In 1953, when Carole was fourteen, we had a fourth child, Richard. He had an even more serious congenital heart defect than Roland had and lived only four years. We were a family in circumstances which occasionally were touch and go, but it never occurred to us that there was anything to do but by the help of God to cope. As families do, we did what had to be done, and refused to engage in futile self-flagellation or to feel sorry for ourselves.

Like a multimedia show of sight and sound, memories of Carole's childhood flash across my mind:

. . . Carole in her blue bunny costume with the pink ears hopping around in her first dance recital at age four.

. . . Carole, hurt and angry, standing outside a restaurant in Knoxville, Tennessee, one arm thrown protectively around her little sister and holding her little brother in the other. Marion had left them there to eat while she went back to the motel to check on me because I wasn't well. When she returned, there they were on the outside refusing to go back in. Little Brother had gotten sick at the table and thrown up all over the place, and the waitress had remarked icily, "People with children like that shouldn't take them to a nice restaurant." Carole, all of eight or nine, was incensed and, taking her sister and brother in hand, walked out.

. . . Carole, age twelve, at a girl's camp for two weeks in the summer feeling responsible for her little sister, age nine, in her first camp experience. When Elaine got a sore throat with fever and was not allowed to go swimming for two days, Carole refused to swim and sat out to keep her little sister company. I had forgotten about this, if I ever knew it, but Elaine hasn't forgotten and told me about it after she read my recollections of their childhood.

. . . Carole, amid her friends in the children's choir, an intense angel in stiff collar with huge black bow, eager to sing well. She had a warm soprano voice that reached out with a soft, gentle touch. After her death a neighbor wrote: "The thing that stands out so clearly in my memory is a little incident that occurred when she was about ten. On a bright sunny day I was grading papers in the yard when I became aware of someone singing. I stopped and listened. The shrubs almost hid the figure from view but I could see it was a child standing up in a swing in your yard. She swung gently as she sang in sweet, clear, childish tones the Lord's Prayer, every note from beginning to end. I found it strangely stirring; and, though I never spoke of it, it has come to my mind several times across the years."

. . . Carole being baptized when she was ten, a beautiful moment for a pastor-father with his firstborn.

. . . Carole successively "falling in love" in high school, involving herself in a healthy procession of adolescent heartthrobs. The inevitable breaking up, producing a world-shaking crisis, was always followed shortly by another boy calling to take her to a movie or dance, and generally making a pleasant nuisance of himself.

. . . Carole dancing alone in the moonlight in a white dress, a lithe night figure floating in circles along the sidewalk. A neighbor later told us about enjoying that scene unobserved. Sitting on her front porch she had watched Carole emerge from her date's car to go in and change her party clothes. As she went up the walk she pirouetted in exuberant, unself-conscious, youthful joy.

. . . Carole faithfully practicing the piano during the early morning hours before the family had arisen, because it was important to her to play well, although she was not a gifted musician.

. . . Carole having the female lead in the high school play, *Daddy Longlegs*, her very first venture in drama during her freshman year. Her penchant for stage and platform already showed, and she went on to play the lead in both *Jane Eyre* and *Pride and Prejudice*. The roles fit her well because she was at home in that period.

. . . Carole as a high school cheerleader—then head cheerleader, a post she undertook with the same intensity she gave to everything. We served our time as parents of two daughters traveling to neighboring towns on Friday nights to do their thing as cheerleaders at football and basketball games. That was one part of their growing up that I could have done without. Carole's cheerleading always puzzled me. She was not an aggressive, outgoing, gung ho person, but a bit shy and reflective, never happier than when curled up with a good book or record or thoughtful conversation with a friend. An enormous thirst for experience, recognition, and approval must have driven her to do so many different things.

. . . Carole feeling good about being who she was, a preacher's daughter, deeply involved in the church's life, living in a fishbowl, yet not resenting it or feeling that to be accepted by peers she had to scorn her parents' faith.

. . . Carole as a seventeen-year-old high school senior entering and winning a state public speaking contest and a $1,000 scholarship, no small sum in the 1950s, to the college of her choice. Subsequently, she represented Virginia in a national assembly of similar winners from various states and territories, all gathered in Philadelphia to commemorate the bicentennial of Alexander Hamilton's birth. Although the week in Philadelphia was glorious, Carole never liked the speech she made about Hamilton because she objected to his politics and his moral life. Hamilton represented privilege and aristocracy. The only aristocracy she had any use for was of the mind and spirit.

Once when she was a college freshman, after delivering the Hamilton speech to a women's club, she recorded in her personal journal: "Today I lived a farce for minutes of a speech I didn't mean. I talked to a group of ladies whose organization is against the intelligence of a progressive thinker—the idolizing of the past. My experience this summer at a convention provided a genuine note of enthusiasm for the words I spoke, and yet how I

wanted to laugh or feel ashamed at all the false pretenses I made
. . . . I blast forth gloriously with empty phrases I don't half
believe. Why do I allow my integrity to be weakened by such
pretension?"

The following fall she wrote some lines reflecting her passion
for words and her constant concern that words be more than
misty phantoms.

> What have I to say?
> My words spoken through
> A maze of magnolia leaves
> Are misty phantoms of reality.
> Nothing more than droning voices
> Muffled by a distant melody,
> Nothing less than squares of sunlight
> On a red-checked pattern.

"Magnolia leaves" and "squares of sunlight" suggest her dis-
satisfaction with any semblance of pretense. This little Southern
girl with soft voice and sharp mind who would have looked at
home in a hoop skirt on an antebellum veranda in Charleston,
South Carolina, eschewed that model because she felt that it
was dishonest for her. Her words must be weightier than "misty
phantoms" or "droning voices muffled by a distant melody."
Nothing she wrote tells me more about her or more accurately
describes the struggle she had with herself to avoid playing
games.

What got her on the "Hamilton circuit" was a speech she gave
in high school about being a preacher's daughter. That "P.K."
(Preacher's Kid) speech earned her the scholarship and the right
to represent Virginia in the Hamilton celebration at Philadelphia. The "P.K." speech is important because it reflects her
intense need to present herself honestly and her satisfaction in
being who she was. For those reasons I quote the speech at

some length, feeling that her ideas are significant:

> All my life I have been faced with the problem of being different. Every "P.K." goes through the same experience. And likewise each of us becomes accustomed to that inevitable remark, "So you're a preacher's kid!" It isn't that we are ashamed of our parentage, for most of us make no effort to hide the fact. But, like every other position in life, being the offspring of the clergy has its disadvantages as well as its compensations.

> All "P.K.s" are divided into one of two categories by outsiders. We are either very saintly and goody-goody, or else we are worse than other people. There doesn't seem to be an average preacher's kid. Of the two extremes, I don't know which I prefer.

> However, my main disadvantage comes from those people who place me in the first category—the halo-wearer. To get to know these people I first have to break down a barrier of reserve which they throw up about their personalities. They assume this attitude when it is first announced to them that I am a preacher's daughter, and its effects are often amusing to watch . . . .

> Have you ever had the experience of coming upon a group . . . in conversation and having them stop in embarrassed silence because they didn't want you to hear what they were talking about? When this happens to me I feel like shouting at those people, "I'm human, too. I eat; I brush my hair; I cry; I go to school; and I even enjoy a good joke. Or as Shylock puts it, 'If you prick us, do we not bleed? If you tickle us, do we not laugh?' "

> Some "P.K.s" will react violently to their halos . . . . Perhaps that is why some of us get placed in the second category— worse than other people. I am inclined to agree with another preacher's daughter who thinks that since "P. K.s" are forced

to live their lives in the concentrated spotlight of observation they will often wish to do something daring, just to put on a show worth looking at. No remark is more distressing to us than, "Well, I never would have thought that you were a preacher's daughter!"

. . . .

On the other side of the scale are the advantages or compensations. Every "P.K." is blessed with an abundance of these. Our homes provide us with the best opportunity possible for spiritual growth and advancement. If ever the love and teachings of Jesus Christ are to be put into practice it should be in the minister's family. Therefore, we have an added responsibility to the world and to ourselves. "To him to whom much has been given, from him will much be required."

. . . .

One of the joys that is singular to the minister's family is the assortment of guests and visitors who find their way to our door—the down-and-out, the alcoholic, the visiting minister or missionary, and best of all, the young couple who wish to be married . . . .

Home marriages at our house used to be quite an occasion. Mother would dust up the living room, and perhaps add a vase of flowers to the mantelpiece. Each of us children, having had our bath and in our pajamas, would eagerly await the arrival of the pair. When the doorbell rang we leaned over the bannister from the top of the stairs to catch the first glimpse of the blushing young bride and the awkward groom as they entered the house. As the ceremony began, we took our places on the stairs and, peeping through the rails, held on to every word until the final "Amen."

. . . .

I suppose it's because we experience so many of the same things that I feel an affinity with each "P.K." Meeting one is kind of like finding a long-lost brother, because we have so much in common to begin with. We have each experienced pats on the head from condescending dowagers from the time we were first enrolled in the nursery department. We've become accustomed to the stare, the pointed finger, and the whisper. And we know that every Sunday without fail someone is going to say, "My, how you've grown! Why, you're looking more like the old man every day. Ha, Ha." I sometimes feel that we ought to form a union to protest such actions.

Well, there's our story. A little of the good, as well as some of the bad. But when they say to me, "So you're a preacher's kid," I'll always answer, "Yes, I'm a 'P.K.,' and I love it."

As she said, that's her story. She had no difficulty giving that speech with feeling. More than most people, old or young, she seems to have known who she was and was only uncomfortable with her identity when she felt that she might be misrepresenting it. But if she had occasions of self-doubt, others saw her as a model of coherence. A girl who had known Carole at George Washington High School wrote of her in the school newspaper after her death:

Here was a girl who lived a life filled to the brimming, who partook of all the good and beneficial things which her world had to offer, and who made them better and more beneficial for others. Here was a girl who bountifully participated in all areas of activity, yet remained a completely selfless individual, who knew only how to serve modestly and gracefully, and without expectation of reward or recognition. She was a girl who had all the qualities often dreamed about—beauty, intelligence, talent, dramatic ability. Yet it was not these qualities which left that profound impression within me as well as all others who knew her, if only fleetingly. It was a certain human fineness, a certain quality of the sublime which resided within herself and which was diffused to those around her, leaving its indelible mark.

The words are extravagant, unquestionably emotional, and generous. But too many people have recorded the impact of Carole's life upon theirs, sometimes (as in the case above) from only casual relationships, to dismiss the words as only speaking kindly of the dead. There was something mystical about this girl's life that moved others toward the good and the beautiful. And it still does. In a variety of ways, even through her memory, the goodness of God is named and acknowledged.

3.
On Being Responsible

You forget too much
That every creature, female as the male,
Stands single in responsible act and thought,
As also in birth and death.

Elizabeth B. Browning, "Aurora Leigh"

On a September afternoon, 1957, we left Carole at West-hampton College of the University of Richmond. Like most mamas under similar circumstances, Marion shed tears as we drove the hundred and fifty miles home, while I, like most fathers, drove the car and kept my own counsel.

Some parents claim they can't wait to get their children grown and out of the house, but I have long suspected that those sounds camouflage the empty-nest syndrome. Marion and I are perpetual parents. We hated to see any of our children leave, and now we impatiently await their periodic visits with their own spouses and children. I believe one of society's most disintegrative forces is the loss of connections between the generations.

Carole's going away to college was more momentous than were the subsequent departures of her sister and brother. Not only was she the first, but the only one to leave town. The others attended college where I was a faculty member and stayed in the dormitories rather than at home.

One expects to admonish one's college freshman to study and not play too much. Sure enough, after about a month, Marion discerned that Carole needed a bit of motherly advice. She wrote Carole to stop studying all the time and go out and have some fun!

An extraordinary capacity for self-discipline enabled Carole to function at a high level of proficiency in a wide variety of interests, including getting elected president of the freshman class. Time was a valuable commodity to her, and if she were out of balance anywhere, it would have been in excessive demands upon herself.

At one point she was close to marrying a young man who finally called off their projected plans because, I am convinced, her expectations of herself and him were too high. He was easygoing and lovable. Carole's expectations threatened him. Later, as a student at the University of Exeter, she decided that she was too organized, too achievement oriented. She sought to restructure her personality. Carole learned to relax.

In her brief lifetime, Carole made many public addresses. If she was enthusiastic about the subject, she loved doing it. Her style was clear, succinct, and persuasive. She never spoke unprepared, but first thought things through and then explained her conclusions to others. Below are excerpts from a talk she made in church the Christmas of her freshman year in college, describing her commitment to responsibility as the appropriate response to privilege:

> If we were to analyze the reasons that each of us is in college, I expect that we would find without exception that our goal is to develop ourselves. We hope to become prepared to fill a responsible place in society, to express our talents in creative work, to increase our own ability to enjoy the tremendous gifts which centuries of civilization have left as our heritage . . . It goes without saying that we will not graduate without being changed in many ways. We will undergo a challenge to our value system . . . . In these four years the

> elements of our personality will be stirred, mixed with new matter, and begin to settle into the solid that is the adult person . . . . Remaining faithful to the Christian faith is not the easiest task for a thinking college student. We are young and impressionable . . . . We reject the right of authority and at the same time crave the security of mature opinion.

After introducing the idea that college students are recipients of great benefits and have appropriate responsibilities, she read a Bible selection. In it Paul instructed Timothy about things he must do to be "found faithful." "Train yourself in godliness"; "let no one despise your youth"; and "do not neglect the gift you have." In her "sermon" she then developed each of these admonitions in terms of the college student's struggle toward intellectual and spiritual maturity. Some of the things she said have uncanny relevance today:

> Discipline and training have always been hard words for young people . . . and are slowly being eradicated from our active vocabulary. We don't want to do anything that isn't required of us, and we are anxious to know the details of requirements before we commit ourselves at all . . . .

> You must not only train yourself in godliness, but accept yourself for what you are right now and show yourself unashamedly to other people. Faithfulness to self is another difficulty for college students . . . .

> The last of Paul's advice to Timothy is that he remain faithful to the development of the talent he has for teaching and preaching . . . . Each of us has something which interests us and at which we are proficient, and college offers the opportunity to enhance that ability . . . . What an exciting prospect for a person who hopes to contribute to the world the best of what he is able to do! . . . At this Christmas Day when we remember the most wonderful of all God's gifts, may we also remember the responsibilities that we have been given to be stewards of what we have and are.

Carole was not an insecure and aggressive female who believed that God got confused when he made man first. She was a woman—feminine but not fragile, emotional but not hysterical, neat but not fussy, organized but not inflexible. And, as she said in her "P.K." speech, she loved a good joke. I can see and hear her now, with her head thrown back, treating herself to a gale of laughter.

During her freshman year she was required to keep a journal of her reading and reflections. Occasionally there appears a flashing insight beyond her years. On December 20, 1957, she wrote:

> On this my 18th birthday the things I've read have filled my mind with dark forebodings. I read in "The Messenger" a short narrative of the evil of the Ku Klux Klan and I remembered how this bunch of ignorant, narrow-minded people had just recently met outside my hometown to assert that they would never have integration. I read two accounts of the terrors of man-made weapons, one a poem, "For Thinking of the Sky I Could Not Sleep," and the other a part of *The Diary of a Young Girl.* I have been reading the latter spasmodically and am interested in the conditions which change these people and form their lives. Anne is already far beyond her age in ability and knowledge. These are all the signs of the times— fear, destruction, prejudice. What solution will be found, I wonder? I know the way, but will man ever find it? Not if he lives an average life.

On January 5, 1958, she reported her delight in ten new Carl Sandburg poems: "I've made a discovery! One of my favorite friends has published ten of his new poems in a special magazine article, and I found them. Carl Sandburg celebrated his 80th birthday several weeks ago and, in his honor, a page was devoted to him in the *New York Times Magazine.* I already have a record of him reading his poems and I have listened at his

feet. There is one lovely description in this new treasure called
'Daybreak.' "

> Daybreak comes first
>   in thin splinters shimmering.
> Neither is the day here
>   nor the night gone.
> Night is getting ready to go
>   And Day whispers, "Soon now, soon."

On January 9 there is a cryptic but insightful note about the
ultimate human folly—self-sufficiency: "The more involved I
become with the philosophy of these predecessors of our country, the more I understand their major fallacy. Man never was
and never will be self-sufficient. Divine in soul, yes, but master
of his thoughts and destiny—no."

Another time she chose a quotation from Gibran about friendship:

> Sometimes when I'm in the mood to be inspired by beauty
> and simplicity, I pull out an old friend of mine and read the
> pages that console. *The Prophet*, by Gibran, was given me by a
> woman whom I admire very much, and I believe she knew me
> well. The strings of my heart are played by the gentle truth of
> these lines. There are some which cause me to ache, some to
> nod, some to share, and some to dream. I have a friend who
> means this to me: 'Your friend is your needs answered.' Thank
> God for her. [1]

Later in her journal she wrote, "Pony tail friend, how do you
always understand and feel the pulse of exuberant living?"

A brief entry in the journal reflects the tension she felt between a sense of duty and the desire to be carefree: "College fills
one with superficial worries—things that add up to the word
'discipline,' and that is all. I like self-control, but I must have my
'lazy days' (Sandburg)." The very next day she summarized that

day's experience in three short, expressive sentences: "I'm pleasantly exhausted. I had an experience with the forest, and I wrote it in my heart. It is enclosed there."

Two entries reflect her feelings for the rights of the black minority, feelings not widely accepted among her white peers at that time:

> Great colossus of a nation, which rolls and crushes all within her broadened path, what can you give to empty laughter? What right have you to stifle tears? You cannot organize a heart into compartments, controlling all the hurt of inferiority. You can't expect to satisfy with minor roles an active, ambitious mind.

> I remember now where you lie, Negro boy. You're crouching, struggling in that southern corner underneath the "platform" of oppression. But now that you have seen and understood the life revealed on the upper side of that glass ceiling, you've begun your twisting, screaming, intense motion towards the air. Beat the upstretched hands, oh Great Colossos. Spit in anxious, shining faces. Turn your back—but not for long—other men will come to take your places.

Those were the likenesses of her mind and spirit.

I have not written about her physical appearance, for that is not what lingers most clearly in my memory. Of course I remember her face and form, but clearest and foremost in my consciousness of her is her being. One cannot separate being from physical form. That, I believe, is what the New Testament means when it speaks of the resurrection of the body. The person as person—not a disembodied spirit—survives death. Carole continues in my mind as the person I knew. Her physical appearance is only a part and not even the major part at that.

She had my mother's delicate face with slender, fine bone structure. Her teeth had been straightened by the patient work of Dr. Hubert Gosney, who gave both our girls beautiful teeth without charging us. I hope he knew how much we appreciated his generosity, and I always wondered if he knew or would mind knowing that our girls called him Dr. Gooseneck.

Carole's figure was neat and pretty, not voluptuous. Unfortunately for her, her legs were more like mine than her mother's, and she was self-conscious about her ample derriere. In one of the letters from Exeter she warned that "the old butt is spreading" from all the good food. Paternal prejudice aside, this was a beautiful woman, primarily because of her lively blue eyes, expressive face, warm and sensuous voice, and her unstudied appreciation of and concern for others.

Unless you had known Carole, there is no way that the last few paragraphs could be taken except with a pinch of charity. But allowing for our common human tendency to romanticize the past, and especially the lives of our lost loved ones, I believe the above is a fair description. My purpose in describing what she looked like is to record as much of the way I remember her as is necessary to say who she was.

There are gaps in my memory of Carole, and her sophomore year at the University of Richmond is one of them. That was puzzling until I put the year into the frame of what was happening to our family. In March of her freshman year, 1958, our little boy, Richard, died of heart failure. He was not quite five, and the years of his life had been a draining, stressful struggle to keep him going. To seek help for him, we had visited hospitals in Greensboro and Baltimore. Richard's condition began to deteriorate when he was four, with undeniable warning signs of edema. One morning he died as I held him in my arms. Our grief was tempered by the realization that every day he lived was a battle to stay alive. We used to have trouble making him lie down in bed. The reason, we realized afterwards, was that he had difficulty breathing while lying down. Richard's death probably affected Carole less than it did the other two children, for they had been with him those last months, while she had been at college.

Some six months after Richard's death another crisis arose. The University of Richmond offered me the chairmanship of the department of religion. In conversations about the proposal I said that I wanted to be chaplain to the university and teach part-time. The president of the university did not think that such a combination could do justice to the position, so we agreed to discontinue negotiations.

By this time I was forty-three and had been in Danville more than sixteen years. Was I to make that first pastorate my entire career? Would that be best for the church, as well as for me? Opportunities to go to other pastorates had come periodically, but I could never quite go. Once I went so far as to agree to let a pulpit committee present my name to a church, then called them on Saturday to back out before my name was to be presented on Sunday. I was not pleased with myself about that; but, awkward as it was, it seemed a more honorable thing to do than to go dragging my feet.

In any event, some months after closing the door at the University of Richmond, I knocked on it. I called the president and asked him if he had found a chairman of the department of religion. When he said he hadn't, I said I knew a good prospect. He asked, "Who?" and I said, "I," and that was that. Well, not quite. Leaving Danville was difficult. One doesn't casually walk away from the kind of relationships that come from seventeen years of a pastorate. We and the church went through a good many gyrations, some of which in retrospect are still quite touching; but we moved to Richmond, and I began in desperation to get material together for three fifty-minute periods a week in three different courses. "Give us this day our daily bread" took on new meaning.

During the months of our determining to go to Richmond, Carole was deciding to take her junior year abroad to study literature at an English university. Duke University had an overseas program with Exeter University in Devon. Carole's lifelong friend, Nancy Bennett, was going on that program for the academic year, 1959-1960, and we agreed to let Carole go with her. Westhampton's dean was not enthusiastic about it and would not commit the college in advance to accept course credits earned at Exeter. But Carole felt strongly enough about going to take the chance on receiving full credit for a year's work, and that is the way it turned out.

After the junior year at Exeter, she chose to live at home while a senior at the University of Richmond rather than return to the dormitory. We have always been especially glad for that year because it provided us a great deal of time with her. Our home was only a short distance from the campus and the place was a hangout for student friends of both our daughters. We served up many an informal midnight snack. Good memories are attached to 33 Towana Road, Richmond.

In the fall before her death, Carole was invited back to Westhampton College to give the speech at Honor Code Assembly. While many good traditions were abandoned by college students in the combative sixties, the honor system remains intact at Westhampton. Signing the honor code has always been a solemn occasion for a Westhampton freshman girl. Carole's love of the college and the high value she placed on integrity are so plainly expressed in the talk that it is quoted at some length. She had kept a handwritten copy among her papers. The speech reflects a mature understanding of the obligation to choose the right as one sees it and to accept responsibility for what one has chosen. With an uncommon degree of consistency, she lived the code she espoused.

We sat where you are now sitting, the freshman class of 1961, dressed in white—silent—serious-minded—a little bit nervous. We were there to sign the honor code. We listened to explanations from school leaders and then filed quietly up the aisle to write a rather shaky signature in a book. For most of us the honor pledge was still an abstract idea. Honor? Who could define it for us? What did we have to do? We wanted the rules. We wanted to know exactly what was expected of us.

What we soon came to understand was that nobody would or could answer our questions. We had not signed a list of rules. We had pledged ourselves to a way of life. Westhampton certainly has no corner on this way of life. To be an honorable person is bigger and greater than any institution. What is honor?

. . . .

First is the maturity to accept responsibility for your actions and decisions. This is one of life's most painful lessons for most of us. In times of decision we often long for the "good old days" when Mother and Daddy or teacher or minister told us what we could or couldn't do . . . . Life has been in the process of untying the apron string and setting us free to fend for ourselves.

It is not only making decisions that is difficult, but it is standing by them once they are made. It seems an inherent quality of human nature to want to "pass the buck." It isn't our fault—we can't help being this way. It all started the day our forefather said, "But God, *Thou* gavest this woman to me to be my companion." And not to be outdone, our maternal ancestor turned to the serpent with a like rebuke. So we are tempted to look for an escape hatch when we have made a wrong choice.

What has the honor system to do with developing this sense of responsibility? It has everything to do with it. Westhampton makes each girl the custodian of her own conscience. The important decisions which you make in college must be battled out in the courtroom of your own reason and good judgment.

. . . .

Taking responsibility for our decisions brings us face-to-face with another aspect of this problem. That is the realization of life's ambiguities. We often long for the days when the rules of conduct were as clear as the health chart our mothers Scotch taped to the bathroom wall. A check list of do's and don'ts— how desirable at times! But one thing we learn by making decisions is that the choice is not always strictly confined to a right and a wrong.

This is the way life after college will be, too. Whatever position you take in life, there will be built-in requirements, expectations, and from there on out you are free to make of yourself what you will.

. . . In a world where ultimate values are often shoved under the daily calendar of events or reserved for retirement days, it is a real contribution to the world to stand for something. This school does stand for a way of life.

Our honor system unabashedly proclaims that there are some ultimate values and goals in life—among them are justice and equity in dealing with other people, self-knowledge, the courage to act sometimes against the crowd, pride in ourselves and respect for the dignity of all people, the humility to admit a mistake, the wisdom to begin again, and the spirit of acceptance and understanding which creates a community of friends instead of just a college of girls.

4.
Exeter in Devon

Oh, to be in England,
Now that April's there.
Robert Browning,
"Home Thoughts from Abroad"

Devonshire and Cornwall constitute the southwestern tip of England, sticking out like a big toe between the Atlantic Ocean and the English Channel, Devon first, then Cornwall as you head toward Land's End. Primary in Devon is the ancient-modern city of Exeter, founded by Romans around the middle of the first century, A.D., and built on a hillside near the headwaters of the then navigable River Exe. Remains of the original Roman wall around the old city abound, and recently archaeologists uncovered ruins of Roman baths within the walled area. Saxons and Normans occupied Exeter in time and left their marks upon it. Among its most cherished monuments is the cathedral with its magnificient twin Norman towers dating from the eleventh century.

What brought Carole to Exeter was the university's splendid overseas student study program. The last week of September, 1959, we waved emotional good-byes to her and Nancy Bennett as they stood together at the rail of the Queen Elizabeth. Thus began what I am sure was the most enriching year of Carole's life. She and Nancy were comfortable together. In her very first letter, written on her third day at sea, Carole expressed confidence in the relationship. "I think we will be happy, we two," she wrote. "Nancy is a wonderful companion."

Early letters were full of the excitement and adventure of two small-town Southern girls encountering another world. In London, after an unpleasant moment with a cross reservations clerk at a Y.W.C.A., they found a friendly hotel and a sympathetic waiter who served them dinner after closing time. "We have literally fallen in love with the English working class," she wrote. "Everyone we've met has been so friendly and so kind to us." Before going on to Exeter they spent a week in London, seeing museums, galleries, and plays. Carole, ever conscious of costs (we had taught her that lesson well), faithfully reported modest amounts spent on these "extravagances."

At the end of the week they went down to Exeter and reported to Hope Hall, where they were to be involved in the full-time study of English literature. On her second day at Exeter Carole wrote home, "Well, the glorious fun is over and it's panic time again. Only we still have each other to turn to for encouragement during the first few days as 'freshers.' "

To the girls' initial dismay, the university officials wisely placed them in different houses, assigning each to English girls as roommates. Before long we were getting chatty, favorable reports of their English roommates whom they found to be compatible friends with many of the same anxieties and aspirations as their own. Early on, Carole began to realize there was going to be a lot of hiking up and down the Devon hills on which the University is built. "The legs are getting bigger," she warned.

One letter reported attending worship at the Baptist church in Exeter on a Sunday morning and of hearing a London minister who mentioned in his sermon that he was teaching in a United States university. "Naturally we rushed up to him afterwards to tell him that we were Americans. We found, first of all, that he is a professor at Furman University . . . . I told him that I lived in Richmond where my father was a professor, too. Did he, by any chance, know L. D. Johnson? Yes! I nearly hugged the man. Tell Daddy that I met Townley Lord . . . . What a wonderful preacher he is! We felt so warm and peaceful after being in a church where the people were worshiping in the manner familiar to us."

Subsequently she referred to that same warm experience, writing: "I surely do wish he were going to be in Exeter all year. The church is going to be, perhaps, the place most like home."

Among her papers was a plain, four-line verse she wrote. Nothing indicates when it was done, but it expresses her feelings about Sundays:

> On Sunday morn the threads of memory spin
> A dream of folks repenting of their sin,
> While humble minister and choir express
> In simple words to God their thankfulness.

While Carole's life was inextricably intertwined with church, she did not always find it enjoyable or useful. One letter, summarizing her disappointment with a certain church service, had the following terse description: "The minister began his message this way, 'Aren't Christians *nice* people?' You can imagine what followed. We're the chosen, we're the content, we're the serene. Pity the masses outside. I think we'll not stop there any time soon."

She stood in awe of her eloquent, witty, dramatic English instructors. "Both . . . lecture for almost a full hour and what they say is well worded, so informative and so filled with good ideas that I am literally amazed. I never knew English could be taught that well." And, later, "These first two weeks in the lectures of my two professors have convinced me of the tremendous challenge of teaching. Why, these books just come alive for me and it's exciting to learn from them. Contrasted to the complacent, ill-prepared teachers I have studied under in many classes, this is like going to a good play or movie."

After recovering from initial adoration of her professors, Carole wrote, "We have just heard an unusually fine lecture from Mr. Salter. He concluded with his pet theme—impressions and experiences have no value in themselves unless they relate to moral problems . . . .

"You have to commit yourself to some set of values and some opinion. You see, we have our own little sermons three times a week from the lecture platform. That doesn't sound very new or original (what I just wrote as his opinion), but it is helpful and refreshing when you read books where people assert the lack of unity in life and refuse to have faith in anything real. Sometimes I get tired of Mr. Salter's insistence on moral values, but I know he's right." In another letter she observed, "He always ends up on some moral issue. Better than any sermon I've heard here with the exception of Dr. Lord's."

That Carole was inspired by their example to become a teacher is perhaps the ultimate compliment to those professors. She wrote that "teaching can be exciting," not only to testify to her admiration for the professors but also to give me a subtle pep talk. I had written her about how much I missed my congregation, how difficult was teaching, and how tedious faculty meetings.

> Your letter made me very happy and very sad because I felt so much the distance between us and how much we love each other. I'm so glad that you wrote of your feelings about Danville and teaching. I realize, somewhat to my shame, that I fell short of understanding all that you were going through this summer. Where I was selfish, it was lack of perception and

depth of feeling, rather than unconcern . . . . I know that . . . the job itself is not the essential problem. It is real friendship and living below the surface of life that you miss . . . . But friends can't be "made," I agree, and I was so glad that you wrote that, because at this point I needed that reassurance myself . . . . Friends come slowly with me . . . . Sometimes I feel so inadequate, Daddy, to give genuine love to other people. I don't know what it is, perhaps an over-seriousness about myself, perhaps inferiority.

Carole concluded the letter with references to the family. Of Roland, "His letter . . . sounded so grown-up." Of her sister, "I miss Elaine an awful lot, too. There's just nobody quite as good for a laugh and nobody quite as lovable." She appreciated that "Mother has kept me informed." She said, "I love them all . . . . I feel like I've been home for the time of writing this. It's a good feeling."

This extremely personal exchange illustrates her capacity to express feelings. Most of us are tongue-tied in the presence of each other's needs for emotional support. And the closer our ties, the more mute we seem to be. We can chatter about nearly every conceivable subject. We can recite sports statistics, quote stock-market prices, discuss politics, repeat the latest tidbits of gossip, "ad boreum." But to tell someone how we feel—not the state of our health but the condition of our psyche—is next to impossible for a great many of us.

Letters from Exeter, in regular procession six or seven days apart, often were no more than newsy, lighthearted reports of experiences of a bright, unspoiled, and unjaded mind visually devouring everything in sight. Once she took most of an air mail "blue letter" to describe a weekend visit to several tiny villages in Cornwall along England's southwestern coast. She had stayed overnight in the home of a couple who had reared and married off two daughters. There, Carole had felt warmly parented. She had climbed down steep rocky steps to the village Clovelly, collected smooth stones at oceanfront, and met a member of Parliament. She had an unerring sense of what was important. "One of the best things about the trip was, as usual, the people."

One morning during our residence at Exeter, a man with graying hair tapped on the window of the room where I was writing. He was Mr. Jackson, and he had come to tell us he had known Carole. He and his family had lived in the house which had been Carole's dormitory, and she had on occasion baby-sat his little boys. We were to come to his house and meet his wife and one of his sons, now grown, of course, and a young woman who had been Carole's fellow student. This seemed to us a singular coincidence, for a day or so later, rereading Carole's letters, I found: "Happy Guy Foulkes Day! Fireworks are going off all around and the little Jackson children who live in Monty have had their bonfire . . . . It's nice to have a family living with us. Sometimes at night when we're making coffee in the Jacksons' kitchen they are in there drinking a cup and talking. It gives you a secure feeling that only the stability of a marriage and children can bring."

One entire letter described a weekend at Cambridge University. Carole's escort was a charming British aristocrat—"Dad went to Eton and Cambridge" type. She was entranced by the centuries of history and the "quaint little bridges spanning the River Cam," and more impressed with the simplicity of King's College Chapel "than with all the cathedrals we have visited." Most of all, she felt like Alice in Wonderland among the sons of England's first families. "It was quite a thrill to be madly gay for a while even though a steady diet of such a life would be distasteful." The "two accomplished Danville ladies," as she termed Nancy and herself, felt a bit out of their social league among Cambridge bluebloods.

She described an evening with a kind American couple who had her to a good steak dinner and bridge in their apartment with an American student named Chuck. "As usual, I starred in the bridge game with Chuck grimacing across the table as I wasted a trump, etc. I'm sure he'd never quite met a bidder like I am . . . . Actually, I usually made my bids. He didn't, and that's what was infuriating." I know exactly how poor Chuck must have felt. In our family playing games is almost a rite of passage. We play about every kind of game, but when you get down to serious gamesmanship, it's bridge. Carole, like her mother, was never much of a bridge player. In one letter she wondered "if Mother is still falling asleep at the bridge table."

Christmas drew near, the only one Carole ever spent away from the family. She wanted us to know that she missed us, despite anticipation of a trip to Switzerland, Italy, Germany, and France she and three other American girls at Exeter planned to make during the holiday from mid-December to mid-January. Her gift wishes were simple: "I would like to have a picture of the family and some of the house and University. Perhaps some book money would be appreciated . . . . Most of all, just send a letter with your love and news about your Christmas. I think materially speaking I've already had my birthday and Christmas for years to come." Without making a ritual of it, she never failed to express gratitude for her opportunity to study at Exeter. And she never failed to link important occasions with her devotion to family. She spent Christmas in Venice and wrote: "It was almost impossible for me to believe that yesterday was the same important day that it has been all my life. Christmas without family is just not Christmas."

Venice, she thought, was depressingly decadent. She was offended by what she took to be a national characteristic of

Italian males to stare suggestively and make advances to all young females. "We've had them from twelve-year-olds hollering, 'Ello, Baby,' and throwing their bubble gum at us to sixty-year-olds leaning on their canes." She was not amused. Nonetheless, she liked the Italians and found them a noisy, gregarious, and spontaneous people. "They always want to start a conversation," she observed, whether they spoke English or not. "For instance, we were on the train going from Venice to Rome and about eight soldiers came into and around our compartment. We all started singing—Christmas carols, popular songs, national anthems, etc., and before long we were one happy group. They took their suitcases down and opened them, and lo and behold, they were full of food instead of clothes. We passed around our cake and cheese, and they handed us a huge chicken leg and thigh and all sorts of goodies. Now, can you imagine that elsewhere?"

Things were different in Rome where they stayed in the Baptist headquarters and were entertained by lovely missionary friends, the Dewey Moores. She wrote, "The Moores are very fine and generous people, as are most of your friends." She found them "so unpretentious and so kind, and . . . it was almost worshipful to go into their home and sit around a fire and drink tea. I knew that Christmas was kept there in its true spirit, whereas mine had not been as well celebrated."

In Rome she exulted, "We are having one wonderful day after another." Of Michaelangelo's *Pieta* she wrote, "It has a definite power and sweetness. The marble is pure white and the face of Mary shows so well the sorrow that she felt." The Eternal City, she said, "shows its treasures casually."

For three days and nights she inhaled the city of Florence, writing, "I hope that I have not wasted any of my opportunities. I'm sure much has escaped me from lack of sensitivity at one time or another, but, after all, you can't feel everything."

Of her last evening in Florence, she wrote, "We walked at sunset along the Arno River, across Ponte Vecchio, and up the hillside to the monument of Michaelangelo. It is a plateau of land which overlooks the city with a reproduction of *David* standing in the center. As we reached the top, they turned on the lights on a monstrous Christmas tree. There was Florence stretched out before us in the setting sun. The Uffizi Gallery and the Dome of St. Giovanni were silhouetted against the sky. On the way down the hill, the lights all along the river and on the many bridges which span it came on. We crossed the Vecchio again and returned to our pension."

Not only was her spirit quickened by the beauty of nature and of man-made objects but also by persons. "Andreas you must see to believe," she wrote of her guide in Nuremburg. "He looks like he has just committed the crime of Dostoevsky until he smiles and then his whole face wrinkles up. He was born in Russia and has a longing to return to the Motherland. There is about him a depression which I usually associate with the Russian character . . . . He was much more amusing company when he wasn't discussing the truths of life." Or consider this description of a farm couple, parents of a German boy she met in Heidelberg: "We found both of them on their hands and knees working in the soil. You've never seen such hands as theirs. They were as hard as nails, and broken skin and nails showed what treatment the weather gave them."

Whether it be an Italian sunset, a snow-covered mountain in Germany, the broken, weather-beaten hands of a dirt farmer, or the priceless treasures of Western man, she was gifted with the seeing eye and worked to cultivate the rare art of simple, clean description.

On the last leg of the one-month holiday in travel Carole

began to be concerned about running low on money. We probably pressed her too heavily at this point. She had heard the "cold-sweet-potato" story too often. That is an allusion to my boyhood when my grandmother sometimes sent my two brothers and me off to school with a cold sweet potato in a brown paper bag. To stress the virtue of thrift I would often recall those difficult times. Soon the children devised the perfect rebuttal: "Oh, oh," they would announce loudly, "here comes the cold-sweet-potato story."

Anyway, Carole was superconscientious about her financial obligations. I wish she could have felt more relaxed about it. "I am not being extravagant," she defended herself at one point, "but I am spending right much money." Then followed a detailed accounting of expenditures.

The subject of money was to cause her further concern, and it is a source of some embarrassment to us that we were insensitive to her needs. In a letter from Paris, she wrote, "Now let me reiterate the money situation." Carole had a problem. "I'm running close." We were slow in responding, I fear, but it all worked out. She discovered she had miscalculated her balance in French francs and had considerably more left than she thought. Even so, she felt a certain heaviness akin to guilt about using family resources. "I have purchased as many things as I wanted, eaten too much, not denied myself any sightseeing or any necessary comfort . . . . In spite of my negligence, I'm very thankful."

The reference to negligence introduces an extra touch of sadness to this chronicle. Because of her rather indefinite itinerary in Germany and because we received no mail from her for nearly two weeks, we became apprehensive and called her in Paris. She was glad to hear our voices but terribly embarrassed that being out of touch for many days had caused unnecessary stress. "Guess who feels like a first-class heel," she confessed in the next letter. "I . . . am awfully sorry about the worrying you did." How ill-prepared we were for the lasting separation just three years later!

Back at Exeter for her second term, Carole wrote, "I'm afraid my attitude about coming back was not very healthy, but it was because we had such a good and free time." Soon she and Nancy were caught up in the excitement of their beloved English literature, and everything was well.

News during winter term took the familiar character of a college girl's report of routine experiences. She had grown accustomed to the place. Friends came to visit. They had dates with fascinating young Englishmen. A letter from a former roommate at Westhampton announcing her forthcoming marriage elicited a poignant comment: "It means another person virtually out of my life . . . . This kind of thing will happen to me more and more in the coming years, and I will be happy and sad and new friends will come. Then maybe one day I will start a new life myself. I hope so."

"Rag Week," a national university custom to raise money for charity, interrupted both sleep and study. Carole wrote, "Yesterday each hall decorated several floats and rode through the town followed by hordes of students shaking collecting tins to the crowds. I had the loveliest ride of all. I was in a bathtub blowing bubbles and completely covered with cellophane and cotton. It was great fun. People threw money into the tub and laughed at us." Students' hijinks for a good cause—or no cause—are strikingly similar on either side of the Atlantic.

The end of March brought unpleasantness between us. In retrospect, it was trivial—not worth one moment's distress. The thing began with Carole being tapped *in absentia* for Mortar Board, considered at Westhampton a distinct honor. We were proud and pleased, of course, especially since she had not been enrolled at Westhampton during that academic year. She received notification that she had been chosen, but was busy trying to finish papers for the winter term at Exeter and delayed sending a letter of acceptance and thanks. Word reached us that she had not responded, and we were embarrassed. Off went a scolding lecture in the mail.

Two letters—painful at points—reveal a facet of our relationship. "I seem to have to begin quite a few letters with apologies to you," she wrote. "I really don't think you needed to be indignant about the Mortar Board, however . . . . I was pleased and have written my thanks to the appropriate people. You know me well enough to know that I was honored and appreciate what my friends did for me."

Our first critical letter had been followed by another. We must have hit her with a double-barreled blast, for three days after her first defense there came a letter reflecting the deepest hurt she ever expressed to us. "I can't be too upset by anything when we're having such a lovely day as this one, but I think I must answer your letter that I received today, and then forget all about it. Being so far away from each other where we can't sit down and discuss things face to face, the tone of our letters is of particular importance. The last two letters I have gotten from home have made me both angry and hurt because they were ugly. I know that the situation is often strained because I don't write as much as I should but it doesn't help to write unpleasant feelings which will soon be remedied anyway by a little explanation."

She was right, of course, and her letter cut deeply. Compounding the errors already straining the relationship, once again we had been dilatory about sending money for holiday travel. She let us have it, properly so: "I thought that there was no question but that I would have money to go to Spain. As it was, it didn't arrive until today, and my bank has had to issue Traveler's Checks on an unapproved check . . . . I'm doing exactly what I'm asking you not to do, and that is writing some unkind things. Let's forgive and forget all this, please. It's hard enough when a strain comes between people who are together, but it's terrible when they're apart. I am unthoughtful I know, but fussing won't help. I'll promise to be good about writing on this trip if you'll promise not to write me such things again. Just don't write if you're mad at me. Now, that's enough of that."

And it was. We never did that again, and neither did she. It was one of the rare times of real stress between us and I wish it had not happened. She concluded the painful letter with these reassuring words: "Oh, I'm a lucky girl . . . . I'm really sorry if I upset you. I love you, you know." What could one add but "Yes, we know"?

A spring holiday through southern France and Spain was marked by a succession of "Oh!" experiences; but once again, Carole was most intrigued with the people she met. From Barcelona she wrote of "our boatman, . . . the finest looking, most virile Spaniard I've seen yet, and really nice; none of these insinuating, ambiguous glances." In Granada they went to the gypsy caves where they witnessed the supposedly original gypsy dances which, she said, "were about as authentic as the war dances of the American Indian tribes." Arriving late to the performance, they found their seats next to the music makers. "My seat put me practically in the lap of an enormous, painted gypsy mama who was the chanter and clapper and I mean to tell you I've never heard such a racket in all my life. Especially when she did her 'solo' number, she was making sounds like a constipated coyote."

Her final letter from Spain adds an important dimension to

her portrait. Earlier she had written me an intensely personal letter about her faith in God. For the first time in her life she was experiencing serious doubt. Could I help her get things settled again? Can one know God as one knows another person?

I do not know how I answered that first letter, probably not too well, but I hope I answered patiently. Were I given another opportunity I would comfort her more, for now I realize more clearly that what she was going through was not only inevitable but also helpful in the long run. The faith she had learned from her parents in the parsonage and pew had to be reconstituted into a personal faith. This is not to suggest that the faith by which she lived as a child and young woman was secondhand. But her understanding of her commitment to Christ had to pass through the fire of her own questioning to be refined. Perhaps I did not offer my daughter as much reassurance as I have offered many other young persons since. I wish I knew what I wrote her. I hope I reassured her that what was happening was both normal and good.

In any event, she answered my letter saying, "I guess I am experiencing complete freedom for the first time from personal influence which has helped to mould my life in the past (except Nancy) and, consequently, my set outlook on life is changing a little. Now don't get me wrong—I have not *changed*. I would hate to think that I would come home being anyone but the person you have always known and loved. It's just that new and wonderful things have happened this year and my thinking has been influenced . . . . Essentially I believe as I always have, but I can't be as dogmatic about it as I have been."

That sentence was a sign of growth—almost always a painful experience—and therefore cause for gratitude. She continued, "Your letter answered logically and sincerely every question I wrote. My trouble is that I'm fighting against the words commitment and dedication and involvement. I associate with some of my religious feelings of the past the characteristics in my nature of over-seriousness, melancholy, intenseness. I know this needs to be outgrown too, but this year is so unusually full that it is difficult to select and assimilate what I think is important and what is merely part of the general excitement."

Recalling some of her earlier statements in church or chapel talks, the words *commitment, dedication,* and *involvement* stand out as hallmarks of what she considered essential to the Christian life. Now, from the relaxing, carefree atmosphere of the sunny coast of Spain in January, she wrestled, like Jacob at Jabbok, with the very concepts which had characterized her religious life. An aspect of intenseness, perhaps even sadness, marked Carole's personality. It gave her an enormous drive to achieve, and made her almost instantaneously sensitive to others. She could be carefree, but it was as if that mood were diversionary and undeserved, something she had to pay for with an extra seriousness about her work and world.

What happened in the months at Exeter and especially during her holidays was that she had been overtaken by a new and exhilarating sense of exuberance and freedom. The diligent accounting of her expenditures was a vestigial expression of the over-conscientious, pre-Exeter Carole. Even that largely disappeared from her letters after the month in Spain. She was no longer carrying the world on her back. How to understand it? Were these feelings a rejection of religious and familial vows? Was she betraying her parents—and God—to feel less the weight of obligation?

Carole's troubling of spirit came because religion was the center of her world. Her life had revolved around relationship to God in Christ through the church. Any rearrangement of the components of her existence would have religious connotations.

The real question, then, was whether this new experience—
"feeling good about feeling good"—was faith-denying.

I cannot imagine ever intentionally suggesting to my child that
the primary virtue is to feel guilty about enjoying being alive,
although I know that we can never fully determine or account for
the forces and feelings which shape us. Evidently Carole was
concerned lest I become disturbed about her spiritual condition,
for she added: "When I last wrote I was rather depressed. Now I
feel that life is wonderful. I shouldn't write when I'm in a lonely
mood because what I write isn't very cheerful to you. Your
answer was helpful and I will reread it when I get back to Exeter,
and continue to think. Don't worry about me, and thank you for
being such a fine father. You know that I respect your opinion
above all else and am always anxious to know what you think."

That last sentence makes me wonder if my answer had been a
polemic, if I had jumped on her and shut off the conversation. I
hope not, but if I had the opportunity again I would encourage
her to feel good about her doubts and wonders, for these were
surely marks of a growing spiritual maturity. I believe that she
had a continuing almost uncritical and childlike devotion to me,
and I can only hope that I did not close the door to dialogue with
her about something so dear to her as her faith in God. In any
event, Carole's life after her year away was no less devout in the
genuine sense than it had been before. Her love of God and her
faith in his care were exhibited not only in her letters but in her
life-style.

The girls got back to Exeter after two nights of train travel
without sleep. "I found also that somewhere along the way I
shared my bed with fleas," she wrote after she returned. "I'm
covered with bites . . . . Well, it's back to civilized, sanitary
England where one boils both clothes and food, . . . but I'll never
regret or forget going to Spain."

Mother's Day brought a special letter to Marion. The day had slipped up on Carole—she had thought it the following Sunday—hence no card, but loving words of appreciation. More than that, she sent a chatty report of what she had been up to, which her mother preferred to a sentimental canned message on a card, anyway. One month remained before final exams and she therefore warned that there might be fewer letters during the remaining weeks. However, rest assured she would be hitting the books, not gadding about, so not to worry. "Your one straying chick is thinking of you and ready to come back to the roost."

She was now having to say good-bye to Exeter and its people. Savoring the final days, she wrote: "There is an atmosphere of freedom and carefree spirit which belongs with springtime, and I'm longing to abandon myself to it, too. Early morning and late afternoon are the most beautiful times of day now. Things seem fresher and clearer than in the intense sun of midday. When I walk over to breakfast in the morning the sunlight seems to clear my vision and I see things very distinctly . . . . Oh, this is a lovely country and I shall miss it."

With people, however, she sensed the ongoing nature of relationships. "They have been good friends and I hated to say good-bye," she wrote of one couple who finished and left before she did. "But these things happen all the time, don't they? At least friendship is not gone when people are separated."

Yes, Carole, life is indeed a continual chorus of hellos and good-byes. Life would be richer if we could but remember that every person is a potential ally and giver-receiver. We must reach out and risk caring for one another, knowing that to care is to become vulnerable again, to give ourselves as hostages to time and circumstance. What we cherish we are always in danger of losing, and almost certainly must sooner or later relinquish. In a sense, every good-bye is an occasion of grief no matter how casual or temporary. Everyone who walks out of my life takes something, and I must be willing to have it so, for everyone who walks in brings something. Thus the balance between emptying and filling, impoverishment and enrichment, keeps being made over and over again.

The other girls were away from "Monty" the last weekend before finals and Carole had the room to herself. That situation was "pure bliss for a change. You know my hermit tendencies." I not only knew them, I sired them. "I've been reading T. S. Eliot this morning and finally appreciating a bit of it." I have her well-marked, paperback copy of Eliot's poems in my office now, and cherish the notes written with her tiny neat script.

On June 10 exams were done. A letter the next day exulted that she was "an emancipated woman." She thought she had done well on all but one exam, and she feared she had failed that one but hoped "that my tutor will still give me a good enough reference for Westhampton. It was a stinker and I just didn't think clearly enough. Nevertheless, I'm pretty well satisfied and can only hope for the best. Don't worry and don't be disappointed."

One last big weekend, May Ball at Cambridge, remained. There would be banqueting, dancing, and moonlight punting on the Cam. "Knowing my agility in such situations, I shall probably overturn the boat," she wrote. She was relieved, however, to remember that the young man who invited her "is just a plain good boy and not the Cambridge ever-so-superior type . . . There are some of those upstanding gentlemen who make one conscious of one's rough edges."

The weekend exceeded Carole's greatest expectations. She was ecstatic over her good fortune. "Thank goodness, there are the genuinely good and kind people like . . . Richard Poulton

[himself a "P.K."] who like American girls for what they are . . . .
I don't think anything could have been a nicer way to end the
year."

She was ready to come home. Nothing profoundly
philosophical was being said now. She was like a tired bird
heading for the nest. "Every day we talk about good 'ole' home
cooking, and especially steak, fresh tossed salad, and iced tea
(hint, hint!) . . . . Well, folks, I'll see you very soon now. It's
been a good year, but I'm ready to go home now. Keep the
charcoal burning in the home fire and the ice cream in the
freezer."

The final letter of the Exeter odyssey began by announcing
what we confidently expected: she and Nancy passed all their
courses and had "no greater worries than finding our way to our
stateroom to vegetate for five days." Saying last good-byes was
difficult. They were scattering in every direction and Carole
would not be back. "I think we just tried to pretend that we
would be seeing each other again."

How would it be, breaking back into the family routine? "It's
funny to think that almost a year has passed since I've been a
part of that life, but I know that as soon as I get home things will
be as they have always been." She closed, "I'll be looking
through the crowd . . . and listening for Roland's soft little voice
. . . . Just a few more days now. I'll take a last look around Exeter
now and then get on the train. It has been a wonderful, wonderful year. Thank you. I love you, Carole."

We met her when she got off the Queen Mary. Whoever has
seen the space close between himself and a long-absent loved
one knows the joy we experienced in having her back. It was
late afternoon before we could get everything done about her
luggage, but nobody cared about the tedious delay. Carole was
home. The family was back together. We drove all the way to

Richmond, arriving after midnight.

Coming down off the year-abroad high must have been more difficult than we ever knew. She would have been acutely sensitive to any feelings we might have had that she was not delirious about being home. Knowing her, she would have shielded us from the emotional low that she undoubtedly experienced at times. After all, 33 Towana Road, Richmond, Virginia, is hardly Malaga, the Alps, Paris, or Devon's green hills, especially when 33 Towana Road is your own address. But I must say, she never moaned about it aloud. If she longed excessively for Exeter, we never knew.

With her other papers—she saved a great many things she had written—was found a carbon copy of a speech she gave at Westhampton College chapel in early fall after she was back. They asked her to tell of her year abroad. She spoke warmly of her experience, calling it "a valuable interlude," implying that she understood that one only visits but does not live in Camelot. Although the excerpts may appear somewhat disconnected, some of what she said on that occasion is quoted here to show how in retrospect she viewed her year abroad:

> Educationally speaking, as one who loves to read, and is perhaps interested in teaching English, the English manner of study was a valuable interlude for a year . . . . The major academic emphasis is on reading and comprehension—not factual knowledge. Consequently, I had the time and was stimulated to read books which otherwise I would probably not have known.
>
> . . . .
>
> I especially appreciated two things about my lecturers—their sense of humor and their devotion to their work. Frequently they could laugh at a character in a book who portrayed a "terribly British" attitude and they could also manage to poke fun at each of our respective countries. Their own

enthusiasm was catching and their presentation made some lectures so inspiring that I felt as if I had been to church.

The educational advantage other than the actual university experience was the traveling that I was able to do . . . . I traveled in a very relaxing fashion with three other girls and no schedules to meet. We went where the spirit or train led us, as the case might be . . . . There are three pleasures about such travel—the first being the sense of antiquity and history which is a new experience for a New World-er who thinks that 17th century is ancient. The second is exposure to the cultural heritage of other great nations and through them to our cultural heritage . . . . The third value of traveling meant the most to me, and that was a feeling of the common brotherhood of men. Even through language, culture, and educational barriers we were able to communicate appreciation and joy and interest with people wherever we went. We found that music is a common denominator, as well as food, and on trains and buses we shared both . . . .

The final advantage of a year in another country is that you actually become a part of a new life. Soon I found myself actually picking up the expressions of my English roommates and laughed to myself at their unconscious imitations of me. We talked endlessly about differences in education, government, religious attitudes, and social manners and I was, by and large, very proud to be an American . . . . But I didn't just think of my roommates as interesting English girls—they were my friends, and this is the wonderful thing about living in another country.

5.
Home—and the Last Years

Home is the sailor, home from the sea,
And the hunter home from the hill.

R. L. Stevenson, "Requiem"

After Carole returned, summer was spent in ordinary ways. Carole seemed relaxed and glad to be home, messing around the kitchen, enjoying her sister and brother more than she ever had—and vice versa—and getting in a lot of TV and ping-pong time in the basement. Her slides were more important to her than us, although we enjoyed a couple of evenings of show and tell.

In September Elaine made the long one-mile journey to North Court, Westhampton College, as planned. Carole was happy to be living at home. I think she felt somewhat like a displaced person in a college dormitory. She had lost enthusiasm for hall meetings or pajama parties or panty raids. She loved learning with an even deeper passion than I had remembered, but she could not go back to being Betty Coed. Somewhat seriously—at least regularly, we observed—she was dating a preministerial student whom we all liked and admired. She and Elaine and their friends kept the living room full and the refrigerator empty throughout the year.

Among other close friends was Betty Jean Seymour, "B. J.," who taught religion at Westhampton and directed the religious activities program. She and Carole shared a devotion to English literature and found a great deal to talk about. When I was doing this recollection of Carole, I invited B. J. to write an impression of Carole. In due time she handed me a beautiful "Note to Carole," a portion of which is reproduced here:

Genuine friendship is always a homecoming. It is a place where we are allowed to hang the hat of our battered but cherished selves without abbreviation or distortion. And because we are always welcome there to "come as we are," we return again and again. A friendship is a daring declaration of faithfulness.

Once we have known the benediction of friendship, we are never again the same persons, for love re-arranges us. In the unique act of another's offering of himself to us as friend, he is affirming that somehow—inexplicably—our being-in-the-world makes a difference that is worthwhile. And when he accepts *our* love for *him*, he is at the same time (ironic as it is) giving our selves back to us, modified and enhanced.

. . . .

. . . The reality embodied in a profound relationship can never be exhausted—not even by the tragedy of death. And so, I have discovered that your presence sometimes gently (as always) touches my personal moments of triumph or despair, enriching my pilgrimage through this perplexing human enterprise.

I am a far richer human being because you entrusted me with your friendship, Carole. And so, my friend, now—as then—I give you my gratitude for nourishing my life and for continuing to confirm the reality of all that we dare to hope is good in our world. Thank you for always being at home.   BJ

What I remember most of that year were the glorious afternoons and evenings in the basement laughing, talking, and watching TV all simultaneously, piled up four or five deep across an old dilapidated rollaway bed converted into a poor substitute for a sofa by pushing it up against the wall.

Westhampton came through with a full year's credit for Carole's courses at Exeter, so she had only a standard load during her senior year. She was able to elect several courses simply out of personal interest. Two of those were in religion, one of which she took with me, "The History of Christian Thought." That might not be considered good pedagogy, but it never bothered either of us, or any of my other students as far as I could see. She was a joy to have in a class—insightful, involved, alert, with neither a need to dominate discussion nor a reluctance to contribute to the shared learning experience.

The other religion course she took was a study of the life of Jesus. I found a test paper she had saved from that course, one of the questions of which was to "list at least five approaches to the study of the life of Jesus; select the one which comes nearest to satisfying what you believe and tell why." In reply she had listed *six* approaches, selecting "revelation" as the one which best satisfied her belief. About this she had written on her exam paper:

> Christ of the Bible is the Revelation of God in history . . . . It is not merely history and biography, but . . . was written by men who had encountered Jesus Christ and . . . is their attempt to show, through the events of his life, that He was the Son of God. The Gospels were obviously not written exclusively for historical purposes . . . . They were, by the same token, not biographies because all of them together do not . . . give us a complete picture of the life of Christ. They are too well founded in historical fact, however, to be merely the mythological tales of a first-century mythological character. Each writer, I think, was writing to a different group of Christians with a slant towards the needs of that particuliar group, but each had as a purpose to show Christ as the Revelation of God Himself.

I quote it here not because it is a profound theological statement so much as a sample of her Christian conviction. While I am well aware of students' proclivities for giving professors what they want to read on tests, I do not believe Carole would have played that game.

Many of us live out threescore years and ten, leaving nothing more of merit concerning our understanding of life than could be written on a 3 by 5 card. Perhaps our heirs are better pleased to have us leave them a generous portfolio of stocks and bonds. In any case, Carole left a great deal of written material, and much of it has the quality of the illumination of her mind and spirit. Her own words have seemed to me the best instrument for drawing her profile.

Graduation with Phi Beta Kappa honors came in June, 1961. The house on Towana Road was full of noisy, happy young people. The ministerial student—Jim—was around, having a foreign language requirement to complete before graduation at the end of the summer and entrance to seminary in the fall. He and Carole were making amorous gestures in each other's direction. They would be thirty miles apart in graduate schools in the fall, so they would see each other a lot. Within ten days of graduation from Westhampton, Carole moved to Chapel Hill, North Carolina, to begin a master's degree program.

She found graduate study to be uneven in quality, and she was more excited by observation of classes of sharp and creative schoolteachers than by classroom lectures. However, not all teachers she observed received her commendation. One teacher of a class in Russian studies "stifled all the kids' ideas . . . . She obviously didn't know as much as they . . . . In contrast . . . we saw a humanities class where tenth graders were discussing philosophy and the scientific method, fifth graders were doing projects in radar and sonar, running Pasteur's experiments and

Mendel's law, and writing poems and doing interpretive dances. It was unbelievable."

Following the first term of summer school she was able to come to Richmond for a weekend. "Don't bother to plan anything except, maybe, food," she wrote. End-of-term exams were imminent and there was the usual panic, but "I seem to turn up again as the conscientious grind in the crew." She had had a date with a seminary student that somebody (probably her family) thought she should be nice to. Her evaluation was succinct and plain: "His whole world is the Southern Baptist Convention, and I just couldn't keep up with his name dropping. I'm sure he will be a success."

Summer passed, and she was back in Chapel Hill for the second leg of her master's program. One September Sunday night she chattered along in her letter about a variety of commonplace but happy incidents. Jim had been to see her the night before, "leaving a beautiful carnation and beautiful memories for today." She had gone to church, "where I feel at home." She and a friend-of-a-friend had gone to dinner and had a getting-to-know-you session. "I liked her very much. We talked so well that I forgot to taste my steak. Imagine that!" Best of all, one of her roommates at Chapel Hill had gotten engaged, and Carole was so excited about it that "my toes stayed curled up for two hours."

Every letter now reflected a mood of contentment—nothing heavy or momentous. She and Jim had gone to a football game, "fallish and colorful, but I was so glad to see him I talked the whole time and missed most of the action. Everytime we made a gain I would holler out (to his humiliation), 'Oh, Jim, we threw 'em for a loss.' . . . Tell Elaine to hide her winter clothes—I'm coming home October 20." We must have been up to our old habit of being tardy with responses to requests, for the back of the envelope of that letter carried the following urgent message·

> Please send checks!
> Please send checks!
> Please send checks!
> Checks!
> Checks!
> Checks!
> Please send checks!

One night she went to hear a "Metropolitan squaw," whose concert she described in one expressive sentence: "She sang a hodge-podge, and my most vivid impressions of the evening are trying to stifle a cough, keep my skirt pulled down over my protruding knees, and her encore, 'Danny Boy.' " That said enough.

Her first letter after a weekend at home that fall dropped the hint that things were not as smooth in her relationship with Jim as earlier letters indicated. He had been with her at our house, and they had gone back together in an old car I had given her. "Jim and I had a grand time coming home, eating and talking and laughing about the weekend, which really wasn't too good for us—that is, speaking of togetherness. We had fun with the family. It is so wonderful to be home and see you all."

A bus trip to New York to see a University of Richmond friend took up most of her Thanksgiving holiday, but we got to see her briefly in Richmond. Then came Christmas and she was home for the holidays which were spent uneventfully after a flurry of excitement in the fall having to do with my work. That fall the pulpit committee of the First Baptist Church, Greenville, South Carolina, had heard me preach and invited us to visit, which we did. They asked to place my name before the church as pastor. I was then in my third year at the university and no nearer than when I arrived to achieving my dream of combining the pastoral and teaching ministries. However, I had a contract with the university and did not want to ask to be released from it. After explaining this to the people in Greenville, we mutually agreed to go our separate ways. June was a long way off. I could not come before then and it seemed too great a delay in their search for a pastor. That was that, and we settled down to enjoy Christmas, supposing that the door to Greenville was closed. It was not.

Early in January the pulpit committee called and asked if I would come as pastor provided they waited until June. I felt signally honored to be thus chosen. I am sure that I never really got over my first love—the pastorate—although I was a regular supply preacher and I enjoyed teaching. After the first year of frantic lecture preparation the classroom became an exhilarating atmosphere, and now I find myself enormously challenged by it. But I was drawn back into the pastorate at that point in my career, and that is how we came to move to Greenville, South Carolina, just a half a year from Carole's fatal accident.

She celebrated her twenty-second birthday at home and, after Christmas holidays, returned to write us that her semester of "trial teaching" for the master's program would be in Winston-Salem, North Carolina. We had called to tell her of the new developments in South Carolina, about which she wrote: "I was especially happy to know that things were on their way to a solution with Greenville. The situation has complicated itself several fold by now, if this is a typical crisis for our family, but I hope that things will smooth out without the troubles of the past. Do keep me posted. I feel kind of out of it all without news . . . . Christmas was many funs as always. I hated to leave and come back to work."

A letter in early March described her amusement at her own

first performance as a classroom teacher: "I found myself pacing and dramatizing, and all sorts of crazy things which I never would have expected." She faithfully wrote out lecture plans, a number of which I found in her notebooks. Dated April 4 was an outline for a lecture on Tennyson. She had put down questions to raise in connection with certain of his poems. Concerning "Locksley Hall" she asked, "What did he predict? What type of literature today often predicts a future society?"

Questions to be raised about "In Memoriam" intrigue me. "Why does he not envy the bird in the cage, even though the bird is spared the pain of life? What lines show that he is troubled by the law of the jungle, in that in life the most fit survive? Does he feel that man can do anything to make good come from evil? What are some of the evils he wants to 'ring out,' and some of the good he wants to 'ring in'?" Her choice of poets, her approach to teaching poetry, and the quality of the questions are consistent with her nature.

The lecture of two days following the one outlined above examined "Crossing the Bar," and in it she discussed the metaphors of the poem as descriptions of the passage from life to death. Concluding this lecture was to be a "Quick review of his ideas and philosophy," in which the following points were given:

1. That science doesn't conflict with religion.
2. That humans greatly influence each other's lives.
3. That life should be lived to the hilt.
4. That old age hath still its honor and its work.
5. That it is never too late to build a better world.
6. That it is better to drink life to the lees and get hurt than not to experience anything.
7. That God is loving and in his providence will provide for us—both life and death.
8. That there are mysteries we cannot know.

9. That the more we know, the more we should be in awe of these mysteries.
10. That we should never cease from following knowledge.
11. That death should not be feared.

I list these as reflections of her literary, as well as theological and philosophical, interests. The summary of Tennyson's thought may well have been something she got from one of her professors; I do not know. I am confident that she had run it through the mill of her own mind. She was continually asking questions such as: "What does this mean?" "Can we apply this to our lives?" Raising those kinds of questions in students' minds is the important difference between exciting teaching and dull indoctrination.

Relationships with Jim were up and down, and she wrote of a "break and reconciliation" that had "brought new patience and understanding from both sides." The week before that reference she and I had flown together from Richmond as far as Raleigh-Durham where she got off and I went on to Greenville. All the way down she had talked about how things were going badly between them. I remember feeling protective and fatherly and saying to her, "If he doesn't like your apples tell him to quit shaking your tree." When she got off the plane, there was Jim. She hadn't expected him and was as thrilled as a child on early Christmas morning.

But the relationship, which had been a good though complex one for several years, was really over. The first week of May brought a letter which was the follow-up of a long and tearful phone call to tell us that Jim had called it quits. In the letter she said, "I took my medicine almost like a brave girl, even though it hurt going down. It seemed terribly hard to believe that Jim who had been so devoted and faithful could have changed his feelings so completely. But he has—there's no mistaking it. I'm just glad I found out now instead of trying to limp along on a half-running relationship . . . . I don't feel bitter and, somehow, I don't even feel too sad anymore. I'm relieved that it is all over and I can breathe again. This week I've been running from the truth like a scared child from the bogey man . . . . Now I am looking forward to this summer and to teaching next year."

A letter nearly three weeks later was written merely to thank us for being supportive. She was coming home to exchange the old "tank" she had been driving for a smaller and newer car we had, but she wanted the letter to reach us before she did. "I am ashamed that I have neglected to thank you both for being so understanding during these last few weeks. I guess I've kept myself busy and preoccupied as a way of forgetting and I just haven't shown my appreciation to you." This would be her last visit to the white two-story house on Towana Road because we moved to Greenville in early June.

She had one summer to go on the master's program and was soon engrossed in being a student again. She called her feelings the "same ole academic thrills which don't last long but keep your interest up." Time out was taken for a trip to Greenville to attend a meet-the-pastor-and-his-family reception given by the church, an affirming occasion for all of us. There was also a trip to Washington and Baltimore on a job hunt. Later she received a contract to teach English at Hermitage High School in Richmond and was there, of course, from September until that December 21.

In July we began to get bright, happy news about a new man in her life. "You'd approve," she wrote confidently. "Nick has studied in Austria, climbed the Matterhorn, is getting Master's and Ph.D. in history—is really cute—goes to church with me—you know—does just about everything right . . . . This is the best fun yet. I'll keep you informed about how long it lasts."

From that time on her letters were full of Nick. Would we be coming through Chapel Hill the first of August? "Nick and I would love to see you . . . . [His father] wrote today about Nick's new girl and her father. If she's L. D.'s daughter, she's all right . . . . Nick is to call them collect so that they can hear Carole's voice. Isn't that wonderful? . . . Please stop by Saturday afternoon. Nick wants to meet you."

We did not get by to see them, but talked to them on the phone, and her next letter exulted, "Wasn't it good to talk to Nick? You wait until you see him in the flesh . . . . And he's so sweet to me. I'm watching those apples, but I'm sure not gonna hide them from the right person and he's the one." She felt a little perplexed at being so giddy in so short a time, but explained it by saying, "The backgrounds' being so much alike made a lot of difference. We just understood things about each other from the beginning—and there are none of those tensions—none at all."

Her excitement was boundless. They had talked to his family, and she had been welcomed into the clan. "Nick has already told them we are in love and the whole family, relatives and all, are talking about Nickie and Carole . . . . So, everything is unbelievably good. We've come down off the cloud now, and are learning to live with each other day by day. That's a lot harder, but . . . what a pleasant task! Nick is really all I have ever wanted in a man and I think the Lord was holding on to me until he came along."

She rattled on about a trip to the beach with Nick; then they were coming to Greenville. Three more weeks of freedom and she would begin her first teaching job for "real money." Already she had plans, she said, for the shekels she would be bringing in. "After you get yours, Scrooge, I have to start saving for my P.H.T. degree. That's 'put hubby through' around here. Now don't panic. I'm not being premature. We're just speculating a bit. Think you're going to be around next June?

"My studying has degenerated to nothing, but nothing," she wrote in mock lamentation. "Life's wonderful this way." They came to Greenville the last week in August, and it was a good time with all the family together. Then she went to Richmond to her teaching job, writing home about how terribly she and Nick missed each other. "You see," she wrote, using the apple tree metaphor we had between us for years, "he's shaking the tree pretty hard and he likes the apples. I hope you will be satisfied with the ole boy. He's going to be around for a long time. His parents are going to get the June plans when he gets home today. Whoopee!"

I saw her only twice after that. She and Elaine came home to Greenville from Richmond to be with us on their mother's birthday in October. That visit was marred somewhat by some strain between Elaine and us over a matter in which I am now sure we were mainly in the wrong. Carole was very supportive of her sister. To make matters more difficult, Elaine had a siege of mononucleosis and Carole, though trying to cope with her first year of teaching, was extremely solicitous and spent numerous afternoons with her while she was recuperating.

There had always been a special protector aspect in Carole's relationship with her sister and brother. Roland has told us that during her senior year when she lived at home on Towana Road and he was a fourteen-year-old, junior high school student struggling with French, he used to go to her room at night and they would sit and talk by the hour, not especially about French, but about life, and he always found those times calming and reassuring.

Nick came with her to our house for Thanksgiving. They were full of joy and anticipation of the Christmas holidays. She was to go to his home the day after Christmas to spend the rest of the season with him. Then came that shattering moment when her beautiful earthly life ended, altering forever the plans they had made. I use the material about Jim and Nick with reluctance. Theirs was a private and personal relationship with Carole, and the last thing I want to do is to embarass either man. Her life was so entwined with theirs that to leave out that part of the story would distort the picture of her. To use them anonymously would make no sense. I must hope that neither will consider what I have reported a graceless reopening of a closed chapter in both of their lives.

Sixteen years have passed. People we had known, and people we had never known but who knew Carole, tried to help in every conceivable way with letters, cards, calls, and visits. All were appreciated, but there isn't much solace save to trust in God's sufficient grace. I read all the messages then—numbed and bewildered though I was—and we tried to acknowledge as many as possible in due time. Some were, then and now, deeply moving.

A young man with whom Carole had been close friends in high school wrote us, "No single person has influenced my life more than Carole and no single incident has shaken me more than Carole's death . . . . Carole lived with such an enthusiasm and such love that she filled her hours and days in a way that most of us are not capable of doing."

From one of her apartment mates at Chapel Hill we got this thoughtful line: "All of us felt that Carole was the best one of us in pure goodness, intelligence, personality, and even appearance." A teacher at Hermitage High School who had known Carole since her childhood told us that she had stood near her at the assembly program that last morning and thought how lovely she looked and how much like Christmas. One of the most touching letters came from a student at the high school who told us that she had known Carole only slightly, yet she had made a profound impression on her life. "At the beginning of the semester, she was my homeroom teacher; however, my schedule was soon changed, and since then I have had another teacher . . . . During my study hall, I am often able to deliver announcement sheets to the teachers. I always requested to carry the notices to rooms 211 through 221 because 221 was your daughter's room. It was such a joy just to enter her room! She spoke so softly, so gently, and she always wore a glowing smile that made everyone feel so at ease in her presence."

A girl who knew her at Exeter wrote to us that "Carole never knew what effect she had on my life . . . . It was because Carole was her warm, loving self who embraced life with a spontaneous joy and who exemplified in an unpretentious way Christian love that I am the person I am today. My heart found its birth in the presence of Carole's beautiful soul—her total self. For me that soul lives on."

Afterwards, we put them all away, as Dickinson said, along with the hopes and dreams which she and we had shared for her. Rereading her letters brings back much that I had filed in the more remote corridors of my memory. I am glad that I brought it all back to the front and went through it again. Though painful, I can handle it better now, and I am glad to feel Carole's vivacity and her keen sensitivity again. From this distance I see her character maybe even more clearly than when she was visible. Earthly immortality has always seemed to me a feeble, flickering candle extinguished by the last breath of the last rememberer.

Is our loss greater than that suffered a thousand thousand times over and over again by others? Does it hurt worse because she was so bright and loving? I cannot say that it does. I can only say that she was all those good things—and that she was ours.

Carole lost her life in a senseless, meaningless tragedy for which I can yet find no good purpose. I accept it and have tried to turn it to good use that it might not remain an unmitigated loss. I will deal with three issues associated with the end of her life: grief, justification for believing in a good God and a rational universe where such things happen, and the Christian meaning of death and resurrection.

6.
The Nature and Uses of Grief

Forgive my grief for one removed,
Thy creature whom I found so fair.
　　Alfred Tennyson, "In Memoriam: A. H. H."

Most of what I know about grief I have learned the hard way. I don't mean that clinical studies have been of no use. I have found them instructive in reflecting upon my grief over Carole's death. Still, what follows is largely firsthand.

Nobody is spared grief. Some may have more exposure than others, and some may be more sensitive than others to its pain, but everybody experiences it. Grief is the emotional, intellectual, and volitional response one makes to the disruption of his world by acute loss. Not confined to a death, grief's essential cause is the sense of deprivation. Moving from a familiar neighborhood to a strange one may cause grief, particularly for a child or for the aged. Loss of job, demotion, or even a change in employment may be a source of grief. Retirement is for many people a traumatic grief experience almost tantamount to dying—indeed, for many a form of death.

Divorce is frequently a terrible grief experience, especially for a child who unconsciously understands himself as the product of two people who by splitting their relationship are tearing him in two. A seven-year-old said to his mother in the throes of a divorce from his father, "Mama, I feel like somebody in our family is dying." He was the person dying, as he understood himself, the child of a particular union that no longer was itself alive. There are as many occasions of grief as there are experiences of loss. But grief is probably most acute when related to death, because of its finality.

Every person, if he lives long, is required periodically to make painful rearrangements. And every time he goes through the grief process the event affects him—wounds him, scars him, alerts him to his own vulnerability, and hopefully prepares him more adequately to face the ultimate grief—his own death—separation from all he holds dear.

We may not learn much from the school of grief, but we all have instruction. Mine began early. My father died the month I was two and my mother almost exactly a year later. My conscious mind holds no recollection of either of them, although I am sure that my unconscious does. My grandfather, about seventy, and my grandmother, about sixty-five, took my two brothers and me—three little stairsteps two, four, and five—to raise.

In my twelfth year the clan gathered as my grandfather, for whom I was named, lay dying. They sent us children out into the yard and afterwards called us in to see his still, peaceful body. Awestricken, I felt cheated because I had not been allowed to tell him good-bye.

My grandmother—the only mother I remember—died when I was seventeen. I was attending college a thousand miles away from that Oklahoma farm house, and it was the family's decision that I should not come back for the funeral. Once more I was kept away from direct participation in the grief-resolving process surrounding the death of someone close to me. A year later my brother just older than I was killed in an automobile accident which almost took my older brother's life as well. That time I came home from college to attend the funeral. There were other deaths, but our most difficult encounters with grief have been losing two of our children. Our little boy, Richard, born with insurmountable physical problems, died at four-and-a-half. He had been a source of great joy and grave anxiety. We kissed him good-bye and gave him up. Then came Carole's death.

In March, 1975, I looked at death straight on. Medical examination revealed cancer. Surgery, cobalt treatment, and watchful eyes of physicians give me hope for the ultimate defeat of that enemy. But all of this personal history is to show that, for more years than I have known about almost anything else, I have been acquainted with grief.

What is it like to experience the death of someone dear to you? I confess to a fair amount of resistance to the question. Am I an exhibitionist who gets satisfaction from hanging his emotional linen on the line? Was this grief experience psychological game-playing to be observed and studied, the findings tested against reported data of similar circumstances? The notion is repugnant. People are not items to be classified or cards to be catalogued or statistics to be analyzed.

On the other hand, if I am able to work through the complex web of my feelings and behavior during intense grief, will I not understand more clearly the process by which I coped with it? Should I insist that my grief is unique, that it is like no grief the world has seen, or is it not more likely that what has happened to one of us really happens to us all? Most of all, if I can understand the grieving process in my own experience, shall I not be better able to help others in theirs?

In deciding to make the private story of Carole a public record, the narrower issue of reporting my grief over her death was resolved. The risk of a psychological striptease must be run, otherwise the universal human experience would never be transposed into personal terms. It has been done many times before. The Roman philosopher and statesman Cicero did it after the death of his only daughter, Tullia, in 45 B.C. He was inconsolable. Finding no help in the many books of comfort he read, he wrote his own. He would come home in the evening and write through the night. Unfortunately the book, *Consolation to Himself,* has been lost to history. Two more recent examples are the beautiful, although remarkably different, tributes to their late wives by distinguished authors: C. S. Lewis, *A Grief Observed,* and Alan Paton, *For You Departed.*

Before going further, I shall make two observations, one of which is so commonplace as to be almost trite. It is that expressing grief is not unmanly. Western culture has severely damaged its men by blocking them from public expression of grief or affection. A man shows his "macho" by going to a football or basketball game and becoming so emotionally overwrought that he makes a fool of himself, shouting obscenities at the game officials and calling upon "his" players to "kill" the opposing team. That is considered quite normal. But to weep at the grave of one's friend, as did Jesus before the tomb of Lazarus, is cause for embarrassment.

The Bible is not reticent about grief and sorrow. Indeed, "He was . . . a man of sorrows, and acquainted with grief," and "Surely he has borne our griefs and carried our sorrows" (Isa. 53:3-4). The prophet Jeremiah, as he thought about the tragic defection of God's people, could only cry, "My grief is beyond healing,/ my heart is sick within me. O that my head were waters,/ and my eyes a fountain of tears,/ that I might weep day and night/ for the slain of the daughter of my people!" (Jer. 8:18; 9:1). Jesus wept when he saw the condition of Jerusalem (Luke 19:41).

But in our society "big boys don't cry." We have shut off one of the vital channels for expressing care for others. In doing so we have created all kinds of conflicts for those who need to grieve but are denied by rules of propriety the means to do so openly. In a remarkably candid and sensitive book about his grief in prospect of his own death from leukemia, the late Stewart Alsop recorded the moment when he broke down and voiced his distraught feelings about what was happening to him: "I began, for the first time in about fifty years, to cry. I was utterly astonished, and also dismayed. I was brought up to believe that for a man to weep in public is the ultimate indignity, a proof of unmanliness . . . . I ducked into our tiny . . . bathroom, and closed the door, and sat down on the toilet and turned on the bath water, so that nobody could hear me, and cried my heart out. Then I dried my eyes on the toilet paper and felt a good deal better."[1]

The other observation is that whereas most analysts whose works I have read suggest that the experience of grief is primarily focused upon one's own loss, my reflection on my feelings about Carole's death makes me believe that my greatest sorrow relates to what she lost. David K. Switzer, whose lectures and book, *The Dynamics of Grief,*[2] have been most helpful and comforting, links the dying of a significant other with the subjective experience of the dying part of oneself. Like the little boy who felt something within himself dying when his parents divorced, the death of a loved one means the loss of a part of the *field* of one's being, composed of interactional relationships with a certain set of persons. Loss of any part of that field is painful. Every man's death, most especially the death of those with whom I am closely identified, "diminishes me," as Donne said.

A minister who has written widely on the subject of grief says plainly: "Usually we do not grieve for the person who has died but rather for ourselves and our own sense of loss."[3] We might quarrel with the lack of diffidence and apparent oversimplifica tion in that analysis of so traumatic an experience as grief, but unquestionably a part of grief is feeling sorry for ourselves. We have suffered great damage. A widow may have lost companionship, physical love, financial security, even status. A child may have lost the emotional support and guidance of a father, economic benefits which would afford education at a good college, the steadying hand of an older partner in establishing oneself in a business or profession. Grieving persons who find themselves feeling sorry for themselves should be neither surprised nor disappointed in themselves. They have every right to identify their grief with personal loss.

Where I have trouble is with the suggestion that "usually" grief is for oneself, not for the person who has died. I do not believe that is true of my experience in Carole's death. I grieve for her—for what there was of unfulfilled promise and unrealized potential in her young and joyous existence. I grieve because she was in love, full of expectation, gifted, open to life, eager and able to share what she knew and felt, and that all of this perished. I am not consoled by the thought that she experienced more in her twenty-three years than many do in seventy. Shall I think of God as some Cosmic Timekeeper, doling out a certain number of years, and penalizing with a fewer number the life of brightest incandescence? Does each life have only so much oil for its lamp, and do those which burn too intensely burn out quickly? I cannot believe that about God. I grieve not simply for myself, although I could not deny egocentric feelings, but I grieve for what Carole missed, and for what others who loved her, or would have loved her, missed. She was not fulfilled; her unripe grape fell from the vine; her blossom was shed before the olive formed (Job 15:33).

Grief, as any human experience, is subject to observation and description and generally follows a discernible pattern. We may suppose that ours is unique, but it is more likely that we have reacted within the parameters of a predictable behavior pattern. This pattern has been described in numerous studies of grief. For instance, Robert E. Kavanaugh in his book, *Facing Death*, [4] lists seven identifiable phases in the grieving process: shock, disintegration, volatile emotions, guilt, loss and loneliness, relief, and reestablishment.

Within a loose interpretation of Kavanaugh's categories I can place my own experience. Initially, the grief reaction to the death of someone close is a form of psychological blunting of the unacceptable reality.The blunting—a form of denial, accompanied by numbness and shock—may take a variety of shapes. As a minister, I have stood beside many a family when they received news of the death of a loved one. Only rarely, no matter if the death had been long expected and even if it had elements of merciful release or the coronation of a long, full life, have I seen no evidence of initial shock. Among the common ways of expressing this is, "No matter how long you have expected it, and no matter how you have tried to prepare yourself, you are never ready." And of course that is true. Often people in the initial reaction to grief will say, "I can't believe it," or "I feel numb," or "It hasn't hit me yet," or "It seems like a bad dream." These are indications of a kind of bracing of the psyche, pushing the reality away until it can be dealt with.

When death comes with shocking unexpectedness blunting may be acute. Persons may faint, the mind protecting itself by blocking out consciousness. People in this initial response to tragedy frequently lose control of their inhibitions as the conscious censor is stunned by the blow. I have heard heartrending cries, awful confessions, and unrepeatable words in these unguarded moments. Once I stood with my arm around the shoulder of a highly respected professional man and heard him in the first moments after his wife's death sob that he had always been mean and thoughtless to her. I suspected that he was feeling unduly guilty, but that also is an aspect of grief with which we need to deal.

When told that Carole had been killed, I can only remember dropping the phone, getting in the car, driving home, calling out to my lost child. Blunting for me meant blocking out most of the next several days. I know that hundreds of people and messages came to our home, that our church was full when we had her funeral service, that hundreds more of our Virginia friends gathered about us at her grave; but beyond what I have recorded here, the period is blurred.

Another aspect of grief which I have observed is that it is not so much constant as it seems to come and go like waves on the seashore. An English psychiatrist who has made a specialty of treating the bereaved writes: "The most characteristic feature of grief is not prolonged depression but acute and episodic 'pangs.' " [5] A pang is "an episode of severe anxiety and psychological pain." [6] This is a phase of yearning for the lost loved one and is marked by the restless, aimless activity which bereaved people know so well. "I just wander around the house from room to room," a widow will say. "I can't seem to settle down and get my mind on anything," another complains. "I've been trying to take care of business, but it's hard to concentrate" is another's explanation of aimlessness. One friend described her restlessness after her husband's death by telling how she would sleep a little while in one bed and then go to another. She couldn't settle down.

Restlessness is psychic search for the lost object of love. We are really trying to find him or her, even though the rational mind would reject the idea as absurd. Frequently searching is verbalized in some form as, "I just keep feeling that she is going to walk in," or "I still see him in my mind quite vividly," or "I have the feeling that she's here," or "I catch myself wanting to show him something or tell him something I did." It is not unusual for grieving people to misidentify the dead person in a crowd or see in another a "striking resemblance" to the one lost. This has happened to me several times since Carole's death.

One of the ways we search is to relive, again and again, the experience of the loss and events leading up to it. I have gone over the events of December 21, 1962, so many times that the day is indelibly imprinted on my mind. I cannot reconstruct the days before or after, but I can almost place where I was any half-hour of that day. If you go and sit with a grieving person during the hours when friends are coming to express sympathy, you will be struck with the painful repetition of the loss experience. It is as if to reclaim our loved one, as if to give some cogency to the wild invasion of our lives by this untoward event, we tell again and again what happened, making sure we get it right. Indeed, one of the rituals by which we learn to cope with the new situation which has drastically altered our lives is to talk about it.

There are well-nigh inevitable negative feelings associated with the death of someone dear. The material to produce bad feelings—anger, bitterness, guilt, or depression, or all of them combined—is more than sufficient in most grief situations. Much of what we feel when grieving stems from the need to place the blame. Someone has to be responsible for what happened. If our loved one died after illness or surgery we may blame the doctors, the nurses, or the hospital. We may even blame the one who dies: "I could not get him to see the doctor." "I tried to persuade him to stop working so hard." All such explanations are probably related to unacceptable feelings of self-reproach. Sometimes people are angry with God because he did not prevent the tragedy. Every person who has spent time with grieving persons knows about these feelings.

Elisabeth Kübler-Ross in an article entitled "What Is It Like to Be Dying?" describes such an experience with the mother of a small child who died:

> She looked very numb, so I said to her, "You look as though you need to scream." And she said, "Do you have a screaming room in the hospital?" She was serious. I said, "No, but we have a chapel," which was a silly answer because she immediately replied, "I need just the opposite. I need to scream and rage and curse. I've just been sitting in the parking lot and cursing and screaming at God. 'God, why do you let this happen to my child? Why do you let this happen to me?' " And I said, "Do it here. It's better to do it *with* somebody than out in a parking lot all alone." [7]

Sometimes an innocent bystander is the victim of our grief-hostility. That happened to me once in a most surprising way. Early in my years as chaplain at Furman University I had an unpleasant experience with a student. He disliked me intensely for no reason that I could fathom. In fact, I might not even have known his name had he not been so openly belligerent and abusive. I couldn't figure out what was going on. Two or three years after he graduated, he drove several hundred miles to see me to apologize for the way he had behaved. Then he told me the origin of his hostility.

Shortly before I went to Furman and while I was still serving as pastor in Greenville, I had conducted a graveside service for his father, who had worked and died in Washington, D.C. The man had been a native of Greenville, and his widow decided that he should be buried there. He had no connection with the church I served or me, but the mortuary in charge of the burial asked me to have a brief memorial service. I was glad to help and did what I deemed appropriate. But this son, a student at Furman at the time of his father's death, somehow associated me with everything he disliked about death and funerals. And subsequently, when I became chaplain at the school where he was a student, his anger broke loose. Only years afterward was he able to understand what had happened to him that made me the object of his rage.

Most often hostile feelings at the death of a loved one are turned in upon oneself in the form of self-questioning and reproach. There is usually plenty of grist for the guilt mill. "Did I do everything I could have done?" "Why wasn't I kinder?" "Why didn't I let him/her do what he/she dreamed about doing? Now there'll never be a chance." I have scarcely known an occasion of grief in which there has been no element of self-reproach.

A distinguished man of letters said after his wife's death, "What has tortured me these past ten months since Mathilde died are the things I didn't say, the love I didn't express. Why was I so dim, so finicky, so inhibited, so embarrassed?" [8] More times than I can recount I have heard similar words from grieving survivors. In the case of Carole's death, I have played the "what-if" game a thousand times, knowing every time how utterly useless it is.

Another side of the self-recriminating aspect of grief is the haunting suspicion that the death of our loved one may be punishment for our sins. I shall deal with this problem—and a terrible problem it is—in the next chapter. I mention it here because it is connected with the syndrome of negative feelings in grief. We tell ourselves that intelligent people don't believe that a just and loving God takes the life of a child to express his displeasure with a parent, but "bad religion" still afflicts us with haunting doubts and fears. The formula goes like this: "I know I am not as good a person as I should be. God punishes people for being bad. I am really suffering. God must be punishing me, or why did this happen?"

Anger, whether at God or the doctor or oneself, swallowed and unexpressed comes out in some form of pathology, often depression. The more than temporarily depressed person is likely carrying a heavy load of hostility and guilt which he cannot bear to own. Good people are not supposed to be angry at anybody, most especially God. So we bury our anger and dig it up in the form of continuing, nagging, disabling depression.

Unresolved grief can produce not only pathological states but psychotic ones as well. A student I knew lost her father by cancer. They had been extremely close, sharing many "just us" experiences since her childhood. When he was sick with cancer, a charismatic Christian group she belonged to offered to pray for his healing. Inasmuch as he did not believe in such practices, she sat as his proxy for the laying on of hands and the prayers, after which she was assured that God promised that her father would get well. When he died, she could not let herself grieve. She shed no tears at his funeral, but she also had no more use for God. As she understood it, God had clearly gone back on his word. Promises of her father's healing had not been kept.

When I first met this woman she had lost more than thirty pounds in a few months and believed herself to be in the terminal stage of cancer. She was in severe pain much of the time, and responsible persons who spent time seeking to help her had no reason to question the reality of the pain. She was taking large doses of pain pills prescribed, she said, by her doctor. She was familiar with procedures for the treatment of cancer and described in detail what the doctors were doing for her.

Something caused me to consult the physicians and I learned

to my astonishment—and subsequently hers—that she did not have cancer despite the symptoms. When she was able to face the reality that there was no cancer, that she was going to live and not die, the young woman exclaimed, "I feel as if I have been born again." She had been living on the shadowy edge of unreality. I was convinced then and am now that this was not a hoax. She was not a girl starved for attention. She was, instead, living out her father's dying. By taking her father's disease into her own body, she was doing for him what the praying and laying on of hands was supposed to do but did not. By having his sickness she was perpetuating the special relationship which they had enjoyed when he was alive and atoning for "failing" him.

I have not seen many cases where grief produced such pathology, but grief can surely make us sick. Grief makes us sick if we continue to deny in practice the reality of the death of our lost loved one. We observe this in the phenomenon of the unchanged room—everything left exactly as it was, as if the missing person is expected to return momentarily. I once saw a macabre case of death denial in which a husband had turned his wife's mausoleum into a sitting room, complete with rocking chair and reading lamp, and went every night to sit by her visible casket to keep her company through the evening hours.

Grief makes us sick if we persist in carrying the burden of hostility and anger, either at others or ourselves, instead of surrendering them to God's grace and love. Think of the lives you know that are scarred and crippled by the poison of a relentless anger over someone's death.

Grief is unhealthy if it causes us to lock ourselves in the past where the beloved person was. One sometimes hears overtones of such unhealthy grief in statements such as, "My life is over. I can't begin again." Fortunately, most people who say such things discover in time that the pangs of grief have receded, although the loneliness and hurt remain, and that they can take up living again. We resume living because that is what it means to act responsibly. Grief is destructive when it makes one less capable of fulfilling one's purpose, when it prevents one from serving one's generation, and above all, when it gets in the way of our loving and praising God. To love any person, living or dead, more than God is idolatry.

Grief can be destructive when it is suppressed and denied. Many a person who, to demonstrate that he is a "Christian," or "mature person," refuses to let himself grieve, years later finds himself loaded with an unbearable weight of unresolved grief escaping from his life in morbidity. When you run into a brittle, hard, unrelenting person, look for unresolved grief. Or if you see a person constantly berating himself, or chronically and inexplicably depressed, or driving himself unmercifully, you may suspect some grief that was not dealt with and allowed to be processed.

However, grief can be a positive, generative force in one's life. Jesus' words in the second beatitude have new force for me in this context: "Blessed are those who mourn, for they shall be comforted" (Matt. 5:4). The ones willing to mourn receive the comfort; those refusing to mourn remain without healing from their grief.

For one thing, grieving gives us the opportunity to deal with unresolved conflict. Perhaps we did feel some estrangement between ourselves and the one we have lost. Perhaps there were unanswered questions, unmade decisions, unsettled differences. Perhaps we feel that we did not do our best at all times. Perhaps there are unadmirable skeletons in the closet, and we are angry and ashamed that we cannot forget them in an unalloyed admiration of the deceased. When that happens we often engage in "overkill" of the other's faults to turn him or her into some sort of nonhuman angelic being. Grief is our chance to deal with all these ambivalent feelings. Grief provides us occasions for expressing our sense of loss and for putting our thoughts about the lost loved one in order.

Grief can thus be a positive force toward helping us come to the point of letting our lost loved ones take their appropriate place in our lives, not among the living and present, but among those from whom we are separated by the mystery of death. Even though we believe that they are alive eternally, they are not here; nor can they be. We have to give them up. It is a fine moment when the grieving person can say, "Well, now, that is done. I shall always miss her/him, and sometimes the pain will be acute, but that is a completed chapter. I must begin again."

I do not know at what point that happened in my grief work. I suspect that the necessity to resume work as a pastor was one of the most salutary forces in making that transition. Reflecting upon the pilgrimage to the University of Exeter and upon the writing of this story of Carole, I know that it has been a time of finishing up my grief work about her death. Something was missing. I needed to read again, after a lapse of fifteen years, things she had written. Sometimes in the reading and reflecting the wound would hurt again as if it were still raw. But I now have a peaceful, completed sense about her death.

There is no doubt in my mind that my work with students as chaplain has facilitated my being able to get on with living. I do not see them as substitutes for Carole because she (like every other person) has her own irreplaceable essence of being. But to share my life with theirs does provide me fulfilling work in which I am able to put my grief to good use.

Grief can also be a great teacher. I said at the beginning that most of what I know about this I learned the hard way. I wouldn't choose it, but I have tried to use it. I have learned about the fragility of human existence, that what we love most dearly we hold by the slenderest of threads. I have not only become aware of our vulnerability but also of resources within us which are greater than we imagined before we had need of them. God's grace really is sufficient. Day by day in unpredictable ways he provides what we must have to make it. Most of all, I hope, I have learned to look and listen more carefully. Kübler-Ross, in the foreword of her book, *Death: The Final Stage of Growth*, describes what I have been trying to do during these intervening years—that is, learn

> . . . to focus on some of the things you have learned to tune out—to notice and take joy in the budding of new leaves in the spring, to wonder at the beauty of the sun rising each morning and setting each night, to take comfort in the smile or touch of another person, to watch with amazement the growth of a child, and to share in children's wonderfully "uncomplexed," enthusiastic, and trusting approach to living.[9]

Emily, in Wilder's *Our Town*, touches me when she cries out to the Stage Manager on her visit from the grave back to her beloved family in Grover's Corners: "Does anybody ever realize life while they are living it every, every moment?"[10] Perhaps a few come close, but we miss so much if we do not try.

I am indebted to a colleague, Albert L. Blackwell, for the translation into English of a moving funeral sermon preached in 1829 by the German theologian-pastor Friedrich Schleiermacher on the occasion of the burial of his nine-year-old son, Nathanael. The boy had contracted scarlet fever and died in three days. Schleiermacher, himself past sixty, had had a very close relationship with this child of his later years, and the boy's death was a crushing blow. Yet, remembering that he was also shepherd of a flock which needed his spiritual guidance, he concluded the sermon with what he called a "Christian admonition" about using the occasion of Nathanael's death to learn anew the lesson of love. He said that he and his wife had loved that child "tenderly and with all our hearts."

> And yet, here and there, there steals through our memories of our life with this beloved child a soft tone of reproach. And so I believe that perhaps no one passes on, concerning whom those who lived most closely with him are completely satisfied when they examine themselves before God—even if the allotment of life has been as short as this one. Therefore let us all truly love one another as persons who could soon—alas, how soon!—be snatched away . . . . Ah yes, let us all love one another as persons who could soon be separated!

> Now, thou God who art love, let me not only resign myself to thy omnipotence, not only submit to thy impenetrable wisdom, but also know thy fatherly love! Make even this grievous trial a new blessing for me in my vocation! For me and all of mine let this communal pain become wherever possible a new bond of still more intimate love, and let it issue in a new apprehension of thy Spirit in all my household! Grant that even this grave hour may become a blessing for all who are gathered here. Let us all more and more mature to that wisdom which, looking beyond the void, sees and loves only the eternal in all things earthly and perishable, and in all thy decrees finds thy peace as well, and eternal life, to which through faith we are delivered out of death. Amen.[11]

Finally, I believe that grief can be an enormously positive force in our efforts to help others who grieve. We do not do this by rushing in to tell them how much we have suffered, in a transparent self-display disguising itself as sympathy. Having been in pain, we know something of their pain, and we offer our strength in their hour of weakness. The healthy-minded griever who has returned from the ranks of the grief-stricken can be a valuable ally to fallen comrades. Not only is he living proof that one can survive the most terrible assaults, but also he may be a veteran with a kit of very useful survival tools.

In a one-act play by the late Thornton Wilder, *The Angel That Troubled the Waters,* there is a fine illustration of the positive use of grief. The play's basis is the Gospel account of Jesus' healing the crippled man beside the Pool of Beth-zatha. According to belief, an angel of the Lord periodically stirred the pool's waters, and the first person to bathe in the pool thereafter was healed of all infirmities.

Wilder takes this story and imagines that a "Newcomer," a physician, has come to the pool after many years of bearing a crushing burden of sin. He is standing beside the pool just as the angel's hand is poised above the waters. The physician pleads: "My work grows faint. Heal me, long-expected Love; heal me that I may continue." But the angel says: "Draw back, physician, this moment is not for you . . . . Without your wound where would your power be? It is your very remorse that makes your low voice tremble into the hearts of men. The very angels themselves cannot persuade the wretched and blundering children on earth as can one human being broken on the wheels of living. In Love's service only the wounded soldiers can serve. Draw back."

As the disappointed physician turns away, another man tumbles into the healing waters and comes out shouting, "Look, my hand is new as a child's. Glory be to God!" Then the newly healed man says to the physician: "Come with me first, an hour only, to my home. My son is lost in dark thoughts. I—I do not understand him, and only you have ever lifted his mood. Only an hour . . . . My daughter since her child has died, sits in the shadow. She will not listen to us."

Is it true that in love's service only wounded soldiers can serve? Are the best healers the wounded ones? I think so.

7.
God of Love and Reality of Evil

Oh, that I knew where I might find him,
that I might come even to his seat!
I would lay my case before him
and fill my mouth with arguments.

Job 23:3-4, RSV

Faith in God's love did not answer my questions about Carole's death. The mystery remains. If God is God could he not have kept the accident from happening? The slight alteration of any one of several contingencies would have produced another result. One twist of the wheel, a hundred yards ahead or behind on the road—a tiny, insignificant detail—ten ticks of her little Swiss watch—and she would have missed the truck that crushed out her life.

I ask myself, *If I knew beforehand that such a loss was about to occur, would I not have arranged for those ten ticks or hundred yards?* Wouldn't you? Or would you say, "Sorry, I'd like to help but, you see, we've got rules"? Why didn't God intervene, just a little, just enough to slow her down or speed her up to get her past that icy spot at a time different from the truck's exact arrival? It is hard to think that God's purpose is better served by Carole's being killed. It is impossible for me to believe that God would not have spared her if he could, and I wonder why he couldn't.

What I feel about Carole's death is familiar to many a bewildered parent or spouse. What justification can there be for such

101

meaningless losses if God is both sovereign and good? If this is not a problem to you, wonder about your understanding of the issues, for it has seemed so to biblical writers, philosophers, and theologians for the last twenty-five hundred years. Epicurus (341-270 B.C.) puts the question succinctly: "If He is both willing and able, which alone is suitable to God, from what source then are evils? or why does He not remove them?" [1] Epicurus resolved the dilemma by taking refuge in a doctrine of divine indifference, holding that God has no interest in us mortals. If God cared what happened to us he would be affected by us and to that extent he would then be subject to our control. Such a god would not be God, Epicurus claimed. God, to be God, must be remote, unrelated to our plight.

Some sincere persons deny the problem of evil, holding that evil is an illusion. That seems to be what Mrs. Mary Baker Eddy was saying (if language means anything) in the book *Science and Health with Key to the Scriptures*: "If sin, sickness, and death were understood as nothingness, they would disappear." [2] But the perils Mrs. Eddy abolished by definition remain to hurt us.

Others, on quite different though no less religious grounds, deny that there is a problem because they believe in a God who orders everything and controls all events. To raise questions about what has happened is to rebel against God. Whether one says, "Allah has spoken," or "This is God's will," it comes out the same! It is inconceivable that God would have done less than his best in making the world; and it is, therefore, unimaginable that a more perfect world could exist. No matter how grievous an event, if you believe that God made the world as it is and causes all that happens, there is no way that what happens can be called evil.

Such a view makes God responsible for terrible crimes. If your child is savagely attacked by a demented rapist will you say,

"God's will is done; praise the Lord"? Should we have asked the six million Jews (and the Christians among them, too) to intone, "God's will is done" as they stumbled naked into Hitler's gas chambers? That is a mindless attitude unworthy of a Christian, for what it really amounts to is denial of the problem of evil.

The doctrine of fatalism is another form of denying the question. *Que sera, sera,* "Whatever will be, will be." We are unable to alter the direction of life, for it is locked into a predetermined course. We are like tiny metal foxes running across a metal meadow in a children's game, our path fixed. Underneath the slot through which we move, we are linked to a chain which pulls us forward or backward. There isn't a dime's worth of difference between one form of fatalism and another, no matter what tag is put on it. If a man is not free to choose but is like the toy metal fox leaping on his predetermined course across the artificial meadow, there is nothing to talk about. What a dull and unimaginative charade life would be!

Or you can come at the issue from the other end. You may avoid the problem of suffering by arguing that there is no purpose or direction in existence, or that if there is it may not be known by us. We are going it blind. If there be a Cause, its name and nature are concealed. We are chance collections of atoms, happy accidents for the most part, bouncing off the walls of existence and off each other like tennis balls tossed to the arena floor from the top row of the balcony. Where we finally land depends upon how much resilience there is in us, how many other objects we encounter with what force, and so on. Do not ask for a reason or an explanation; there is none. *Why* is an irrelevant adverb. Our lives are spent in a frantic arranging of odds and ends of haphazard experience into a manual for survival.

The two views, that life is totally predetermined or that it is totally haphazard, are equally unacceptable in Scripture. Further, although they appear to approach the question of the meaning of God and man from opposite poles, they end close together. Life is purposeless if we are not purposeful participants.

All these proposals—too pat, too simplistic—do not correspond with biblical faith. Perhaps we may come closer to a satisfactory understanding of the mystery of evil by examining the biblical view. Primary to Israel's understanding of her relationship with God was the concept of covenant, an agreement in which God blessed his people when they were obedient and punished them when they were not. Israel saw herself as chosen to be instrumental in blessing the world. Such privilege carried greater responsibility to be faithful to God's law than others had—*noblesse oblige.*

The classic statement of the covenant idea, carrying blessing or cursing in response to Israel's obedience or disobedience, is found in Deuteronomy 28. There the terms of reward and retribution are reviewed in detail and the promise made that God will do what he says. When the people stray they may expect punishment, and if they repent and return to him, the Lord will also change his mind toward them and bless them. The covenant formula provides a basis for the theological interpretation of Israel's history by her prophets and historians. The glory of David and Solomon were understood to have been God's reward for covenant faithfulness, and the steadily declining position of the nation after those two leaders was seen as God's punishment for sin. For example, at the end of the seventh century B.C., Jeremiah gave this explanation of the disaster of the Babylonian Exile: "Have you not brought this upon yourself/ by forsaking the Lord your God?" (Jer. 2:17).

If the covenant explains Israel's history, does it also explain an individual's history? Are individual persons under the covenant arrangement with God? Two prophets of the seventh and sixth centuries B.C., Jeremiah and Ezekial, said so specifically. Both attacked a sacred proverb which expressed covenant solidarity: "The fathers have eaten sour grapes,/ and the children's teeth are set on edge" (Jer. 31:29; Ezek. 18:2). No, these prophets argued, "everyone shall die for his own sins." He who does right will live; he who does wrong and does not repent will die. The penitent man will save his life but cannot by his repentance save his children anymore than his wickedness will condemn his children. Clearly this is an extension of the covenant to the individual. Indeed, Jeremiah saw the making of a new covenant, "not like . . . my covenant which they broke, . . . but . . . I will write it upon their heart" (Jer. 31:33–34).

Shall we say, then, that whatever happens to one who has the "covenant written upon his heart" is God's response to that person's obedience or disobedience? Some of Israel's people thought so. Wrote one such poet: "I have been young, and now am old;/yet I have not seen the righteous forsaken/or his children begging bread" (Ps. 37:25). Extend the thought to its inescapable conclusion, and you equate the prosperous and healthy with the good, the poor and infirm with the wicked. On that line of reasoning we white, middle-class Americans are the world's most godly people except the Arab oil sheiks.

Such an interpretation of the relationship between God and his people—in the name of holy Scripture—violates not only common sense but also the Scripture itself. Do note that there is a profound difference between saying that we are punished for and by our sins and saying that we can equate the measure of our freedom from the ills that afflict others with the degree of our being "right with God." There is also a world of difference between saying, "I believe in God and accept his will" and saying, "Whatever happens is his will."

The book of Job, about which I have written before,[3] passionately attacks as a patent impiety the simplistic equation of reward and retribution. Job's case destroys the argument, for he was a man without moral flaw (Job 1:1; 2:3), who nonetheless suffered outrageous wrongs. He who had everything was reduced to a pitiable, broken figure sitting on a dung heap still praising the Lord.

Then came three pious, self-righteous fellows who wished to do Job a favor by leading him to repent so that God could restore him. They could tell him exactly what was wrong and how to set it right: "If you will seek God/and make supplication to the Almighty,/if you are pure and upright,/surely then he will rouse himself for you,/and reward you with a rightful habitation" (Job 8:5–6). Their attitudes and words were insufferably judgmental and dogmatic. They had intellectualized the problem and come up with a simple formula: Since God rewards the righteous and punishes the wicked, and since Job was suffering dreadfully, it was easy to see that he was a particularly wicked sinner.

One should understand that Job's theology was built upon the same reward-retribution model as that of his friends. And because he knew that he had done nothing to merit such suffering, he was perplexed, and subsequently outraged at God.

Without the three "comforters" he might have swallowed his anger at a God who indifferently allowed such sport to be made with a good man's life. But their self-righteous and vindictive attacks in support of a bad theology goaded him into astonishing denunciations of God. He who had been faultless became a bitter rebel, an angry, defiant hero, shouting and shaking his fist at the Almighty and challenging God to come down out of the cosmic silence and defend himself: "Here is my record. See, here I sign my name to the list of my virtues. Let the Almighty set beside it the bill of indictment against me!" (see Job 31:35).

In Job's rebellion God came to him. Rebellion is an acknowledgment of relationship, anger a form of love. God can deal with our doubts better than he can bear our proud rectitude. It is true that God rebuked Job for presuming to know more than he could know. The Almighty invited him, after reviewing some of the majestic mysteries of the universe, to try his hand at being God: If you would like to play God, come and sit on the throne (Job 40:10–14).

Job saw his error and repented. What was his fault? Presumptuousness in the face of the Mystery. Had not the three friends also been presumptuous? Yes, more so than Job, for they had presumed to speak for God. Job only protested what he conceived to be God's unfairness. "My wrath is kindled against you," God said to the three, "for you have not spoken of me what is right, as my servant Job has" (Job 42:7). That is a remarkable verse. Job the rebel became Job the priest to pray for the forgiveness of the three theologians' presumptuous sin of misrepresenting God.

We live by faith, says the book of Job, and faith is surrounded by mystery. Do not presume, therefore, to "explain the ways of God." The god explained by your theology or your quotations of selected Bible verses is not God. We know him by faith, but we see in a mirror dimly. It is only after we have passed through the doorway of death that we shall see face to face. Then faith will be fulfilled in knowing, but now it remains faith by which we see God.

Anyone who has read the book will have sensed that Job did not get all his questions answered. For instance, there is no word of fatherly love. Again, while intimations of a life after death are found in the book, there is no assurance of it (cf. Job

7:6–10; 14:7–22; 17:11–16). Job raised the hope of life everlasting, but he could not bring himself to embrace it.

One other aspect of the problem of God and human suffering must be noted in Job. Three passages—9:33; 16:18–19; 19:23–27—voice the need for someone to "stand up" for Job, take his side with the Almighty. Who is this umpire—witness—redeemer? Is this a foregleam of Christ? I believe that it is. Though dimly seen, Job perceived that man must have someone other than himself to commend him to God. We must be careful here not to think of God as the Cosmic Enemy looking for an opportunity to do us in. That is a gross caricature of the New Testament view of God. It was *God* who "so loved the world that he gave his only Son" (John 3:16). If there is any Christology in Job, and I believe that there is, it is at best a hint of a preparation for the coming of Messiah.

Job is the Old Testament's premier statement about unmerited suffering in a world created and presided over by a righteous and just God. It offers no facile answer. We are reminded that God is God and that those who presume to understand and explain God are more reprehensible than those who rail at him. But railing is also a form of presumption, because it assails God for not running his business to suit us. There is much more to be said about the God of love and the existence of evil than is found in the book of Job, but you have to get to the Gospels to find anything that goes beyond it.

If the righteous sufferer did not deserve what he got, what other explanation might be given for it? Some argue that suffering is sent by God as a test of faith. What about Abraham, being instructed to sacrifice his only child, Isaac? Was that not to test his faith? Whatever meaning we give to the sacrifice of Isaac (and it has powerful meaning) must not make God responsible for an inexcusable sadistic act. Abraham, living among people who practiced child sacrifice, believed that fidelity to God demanded that he give no less than his pagan neighbors, even if it were his beloved only child. We may admire his complete devotion to the Lord and be touched by the lengths to which he was willing to go, without laying on God the ugly charge of ordering a father to murder his little boy. We lock up parents so dangerously insane as to attempt such a thing.

Life's trials are just that, trials. They test our mettle to prove whether or not we are hardened steel or inferior alloy. It is one thing to recognize that we are tested by the buffeting we suffer but quite another to argue that God puts these things on us just to see if we will bend or break. What kind of father inflicts pain only to see how high his child's pain threshold is?

Someone will doubtless say, But what about the petition of the Lord's Prayer, "Lead us not into temptation, but deliver us from evil"? The petition seems to suggest that God is doing just what I have called out of character, but it is not. If we think of testing as a form of teaching, we have a different feeling about the matter. A parent may be trying to teach a child the multiplication table. To do this he may subject the child to what may seem to his childish mind an endless, dull recitation of his numbers. Or consider that the parent may have aspirations for his son to become a weightlifter. Now the only way to learn to lift weights is to lift them. It requires endless testing of our strength and agility against a steadily increasing volume of weight. The petition in the Lord's Prayer about testing means plainly, Do not push us beyond our capacity. In short, Don't give us heavier weights than we can lift at this stage in our spiritual development. Jesus said, "Your Father knows what you need before you ask him" (Matt. 6:8), so the petition is not offered for God's benefit but for ours. It is a way of acknowledging our frailty.

The idea of development suggests still another explanation of undeserved suffering which will be found in both the Old and New Testaments. Hardship, said the biblical writers, may be God's way of instructing us. One may find this view expressed forcefully by the author of the letter to the Hebrews. As a means of encouraging believers who are suffering unjust persecution, he quoted from the Proverbs, "For the Lord [disciplines] him whom he loves" (Prov. 3:12), and then applied the test to their current condition, "It is for discipline that you have to endure" (Heb. 12:7). This writer made the astonishing statement that Jesus himself had to attend the school of hard knocks! "Although he was a Son, he learned obedience through what he suffered" (Heb. 5:8). That is a mind-boggling piece of theology.

We have been looking at views of suffering which are expressed in Scripture. Such are the doctrine of reward-retribution embodied in the covenant concept, the doctrine of individual accountability as found especially in Jeremiah and Ezekiel, the doctrine of the sovereignty of God and the ultimate mystery of his ways with man as expressed in Job, and two subsequent doctrines of suffering as testing and/or teaching. Now as far as the Christian is concerned, each of these is taken seriously because it has a place in Scripture. But each is a *partial* view, and none fully satisfies our wondering minds and aching hearts.

How did Jesus see the issue of the meaning of suffering? One thing is plain: He rejected out of hand the doctrine that suffering always indicates sin, that one always gets what he deserves. The Gospels are a running commentary of Jesus' efforts to heal and comfort. People pressed upon him with their hurts and anguish. Never did he say, "Too bad, you have it coming to you, so I won't undo my Father's work of retribution."

Once he made reference to two contemporary tragedies as illustrations of the fallacy of equating misfortune with wickedness. Pilate, the Roman governor, had set his soldiers upon some Galileans worshiping in Jerusalem and killed them. Also, a tower had fallen on eighteen other men and killed them. Here were two classic cases of evil, one produced by men (Pilate and his storm troopers) and the other by an "act of God." Were these divine judgments upon the people who lost their lives? No, said Jesus, you who suspect that they deserved it are as great sinners as they were (Luke 13:1–5). On another occasion Jesus, confronted by a man born blind, was asked by his disciples, "Master, who did sin, this man or his parents, that he should be born blind?" Jesus cut off useless speculation by saying simply, "Neither" (John 9:1 ff., KJV). God has no favorites; Jesus said: "He makes his sun rise on the evil and the good, and sends rain on the just and on the unjust" (Matt. 5:45).

Do note that there is no suggestion of moral indifference in Jesus' actions and words. He was not implying that sin doesn't matter or that it isn't punished. Indeed, one case is reported in which there was a direct connection between a man's sin and his suffering. To a paralytic Jesus said, "My son, your sins are forgiven . . . . Rise, take up your pallet and walk" (Mark 2:5,9). We may indeed bring suffering and death upon ourselves, but that does not cover all cases of misfortune. If we are to blame for our own suffering, as in some cases we surely are and in others we clearly are not, God is able and willing to help us in our distress.

We have not cleared up the mystery of undeserved suffering. I am not helped by being reminded that none of us is deserving. Quite so, but how does that bring us nearer resolution of the problem? If we are a basket of apples, all with rotten spots, would a sensible person discard the best apples and save the worst? If we are all a little bad, is it not logical that the less bad would fare better than the very bad?

The apostle Paul nowhere explained the mystery of undeserved suffering. He said, rather, that it need not be wasted.
"We know that in everything God works for good with those
who love him," he wrote (Rom. 8:28). Paul was talking about
God's aid in bringing good out of every event of life. There is no
suggestion that everything which happens to "those who love
the Lord" is for their good, or that God wanted it to happen. He
does work with us to make good come from what happens, to
discover the "saving possibility" in it. I can relate to that, for it is
precisely what I understand to be the main purpose of creative
living—to take what comes in all its shapes, sizes, and colors,
and make something good out of it. In that kind of project we do
indeed have God's aid.

In the same context, Paul wrote that he considered "the suf-
ferings of this present time are not worth comparing with the
glory that is to be revealed to us" (Rom. 8:18). His eyes were so
fastened on the next age, to which this is only a prelude, that he
would not allow himself to be preoccupied with what was happening to him here. We have reversed the priority. We spend all
our energy dressing up the anteroom with no thought for the
rest of the house. Doubtless that is because we enjoy where we
are in the anteroom and are not so sure about what lies beyond
it. Paul's reminder about the comparative value of the two parts
of our existence is a valuable corrective to our excessive concern
with the present.

The words also provide encouragement to those of us who
have lost loved ones whose potential was unrealized through
premature death. If this were the only theater of human existence, how terrible and dreadful would be the loss of such
promise-filled lives. If there is to be any final resolution of this
problem, it must be beyond death. Therefore, we who believe in
God share Paul's conviction about the glory that is to be re-

vealed. If this life is only the prelude to the one beyond the grave, then perhaps we can better accept the brevity of a prelude such as Carole's.

But Paul's argument is still no answer to the mystery. The apostle came near to saying, "Don't worry excessively about it; it's not that important." However, one should not make the mistake of drawing such a conclusion about Paul's attitude toward suffering. He certainly took his own suffering seriously and dedicated it to the Lord (cf. 2 Cor. 12:7–10; Phil. 1:12–24; 2:25–28).

The mystery of unmerited suffering remains. I know of no satisfactory explanation. But for the Christian there is an answer—not an explanation. The Christian sees God's urgent work of justification of himself as Creator to have taken place in the incarnation, death, and resurrection of his Son through whom God showed himself to be Redeemer. God in Christ took our sin and suffering upon himself. He has not abolished the hurts of human existence, but he has shared them and identified himself with our plight. He did not change the order of the universe to make evil impossible and thus destroy man's humanity by taking away his freedom. Instead he partook of the cup of suffering himself and gave us the promise that nothing in all creation can separate us from his love.

P. T. Forsyth, an English clergyman of the World War I era, wrote in 1917 a remarkably clear and stirring book on this very point. It is entitled *The Justification of God*.[4] Forsyth rejected outright the optimism which pictured mankind as moving on an upward-bound escalator toward perfection. God had acted in Christ to redeem man in his sin, but he had not banished either sin or suffering. Both were present and always would be in the world. But by his death and resurrection Christ had subdued them. "It is not really an answer to a riddle but a victory in a battle," [5] Forsyth wrote. "We do not see the answer; we trust the Answerer, and measure by Him. We do not gain the victory; we are united with the Victor." [6]

What, then, can I believe about the God of love and the reality of evil? I believe that God's nature is perfect wisdom, power, knowledge, and love. It is inconceivable that he should be overthrown or that he should do evil. The Bible acknowledges the presence of evil, but it nowhere supports the notion that there are two supreme forces in the universe—good and evil. However evil came to be, God clearly could have made a world in which neither natural nor moral evil could have happened. Such a world would have been different from the one we know, for if God is God, his creative options were practically limitless.

But could he have made a better world? If so, why didn't he? Could he have made a world where life does not survive by devouring other life—from plants to lower animals, from lower to higher, and from higher to man? Life on planet Earth is structured so that any form of life maintains itself at the expense of other life. Could God have created a world where natural disasters—storms, floods, earthquakes—did not terrorize and destroy? Could God have made a world where rain came only when and in the proper amount needed? Could God have made a world where disease did not afflict us? Think, for example, what a blessing it is for parents not to have to fear polio anymore because of the vaccine. Why didn't God make a world where the vaccine was unnecessary? Suppose the race were to be delivered of the specter of cancer.

Why did God create this particular order and not another? I do not know, but I believe that he did not create the world as the result of a whim, or out of a perverted sense of humor, or because he was bored and lonely. I think he created the world as a place for persons to grow into Godlikeness. This world is a "vale of soul-making." [7] God's first concern is what is best for persons, not for law and order. He could have created another kind of universe, but he has willed to create one in which it is better for him to permit evil and sin than not to permit them.

Not only did God create; he is creating. "My Father is still working," Jesus said (John 5:17). Creation is not a static and completed act, but a continuing process. Stars are being born and stars are dying in the cosmic time sequence. God is working his purpose out, not only in the human order but also in the natural order. The creative process is not evolutionary in the popular sense of the term, for the process is not a natural or inevitable development. It is under the watchful eye of a divine Father. Further, the dynamic relationship between Creator and creation affects the process. The Bible says that God changed his plans from time to time in response to the obedience or disobedience of his people. After all, that is the meaning of the Flood. God wiped the slate almost clean and began with a tiny remnant—one man's family. (Later he repented for causing the flood and said he would never do it again.)

Evil in human existence is both a natural phenomenon and a human (moral) one. Clearly there are evils (such as cyclones and earthquakes) which are not caused by human sin but still hurt, maim, and kill humans. Moral evil, on the other hand, is the injury persons do to other persons or to themselves to block the fulfillment of God's purpose. We do not think of natural evil as morally reprehensible, although we fear it and seek to ward it off. However, natural evil may be caused or heightened by moral evil. Farmers cut the trees, rip up the sod, and in time get a "dust bowl." Human greed and filth pollute the rivers and lakes until they no longer are fit for drinking, bathing, or fishing. The two realms impinge where the human factor is introduced, and the human capacity for moral evil is limited only by human imagination.

One need not search far for an explanation of much of our hurt. We do it to ourselves. Or we have it done to us by another, either intentionally or accidentally.

Such accidents as took Carole's life take fifty thousand American lives each year. In half of them beverage alcohol is a factor. In those cases only the innocent victims have cause to ask, "Why?" Other accidents are caused by carelessness or reckless disregard for human life.

But some accidents just happen. That seems to have been the nature of Carole's accident. It was no less fatal and permanent than if we could have blamed somebody. Could God have prevented it? Yes, since he is God. Why didn't he? I do not know. I live with the mystery, knowing that what happened to Carole and her family is so much a part of the human tragedy as not to merit space in the obituary notices save in the tiny circles in which we all live our lives, experience our joys, and weep our tears. Does God rejoice and weep with us? Yes, I believe he does.

Reference was made earlier to Friedrich Schleiermacher's sermon at the grave of his nine-year-old son, Nathanael. In the sermon the grieving father mentions two "consolations" offered him by kindly and sympathetic parishioners. One, he said, "is the consolation that children who are taken away young are in fact delivered from all the dangers and temptations of this life and are early rescued into the sure Heaven . . . . But, in fact, this consolation does not want to take with me, I being the way I am." Why, he said, should he want to see his son deprived of the opportunity to live and enjoy "the blessings of the Christian community? . . . . Therefore, this way of thinking is not as consoling to me as it is to many others." Still others, Schleiermacher said, "generate their consolation . . . out of an abundance of attractive images in which they represent the everlasting community . . . and the more these images fill the soul, the more all the pains connected with death are stilled. But for the man who is too greatly accustomed to the rigors and cutting edges of thinking, these images leave behind a thousand unanswered questions." [8]

Well-intentioned platitudes about God knowing best and making no mistakes leave me comfortless, too. "Explanations," no matter how sincere, rarely console. Schleiermacher ended his sermon with a plea to love one another and gave a beautiful prayer in which there is found this moving petition: "Make even this grievous trial a new blessing for me in my vocation." That last is true consolation—with God's help to turn your trials into new blessings in your vocation.

James Moffatt has an inspired translation of one of Paul's statements: "Pagans waste their pains." Let nothing be wasted of all the variegated experiences of our lives. From the standpoint of those of us who loved Carole, it is a good word. Let us not waste this grief. But what of it from Carole's standpoint? What can compensate her for the loss of experiences she did not live to know?

8.
Where Are You, Carole?

Death and Resurrection: A Christian Interpretation

Sitting around the dining table shared by the people on our hall at the University of Exeter, we were listening to a past-middle-aged Englishwoman who if you flattened her *a* and slowed her tempo would have been a dead ringer for her counterpart in Peoria. Her provincialism was no less tiresome nor her omniscient manner less annoying. She sensed she was losing me as I was making unmistakable signs of retreat.

"And what are you doing here all the way from the States?" she asked to draw me back to her monologue. "It's a bit hard to explain," I fumbled, "but the general idea is to write something about the meaning of death."

Awkward silence momentarily prevailed. The young couple at the end of the table did a double take as if to ask, "Did we hear that old man correctly?"

Mrs. Hoighty (or was it Toighty?), quickly recovering, said somewhat lamely, "Oh? I wouldn't have supposed there is any."

"We shall see," I said, and someone rescued us by turning the conversation to weightier matters, namely, the comparative dullness of American baseball as presently played and English cricket as played for centuries.

118

D-E-A-D is today's most obscene four-letter word. Nice people do not use it, especially about anybody they know. People we care for don't die; they pass away. Euphemisms cover our dread. The mortician cooperates with this grief-denying conspiracy by dressing up death to look like sleep, and by covering the raw wound of the open grave with artificial grass—an unintended symbol of the artificiality of this society's ritual for the dead. The minister, likely as not, contributes to the litany of make believe by reciting some pretty but deceptive lines such as, "There is no death! The stars go down to rise upon some other shore." [1]

British anthropologist Geoffrey Gorer in an impressive book entitled *Death, Grief, and Mourning* argues that as sex was unmentionable among the Victorians, death has become so for us. "The 'pornography of death,' whether it be furtively enjoyed or self-righteously condemned," Gorer writes, "manifests an irrational attitude towards death and a denial of mourning." [2]

Prompted by his grief over the loss of his father in the sinking of the *Lusitania* during the early days of World War I, the heavy burden of having to "be a man" when he was only a boy, and the subsequent death of his younger brother from cancer, Gorer set out to discover how other people managed. His own family had not faced death with healthy attitudes. His deceased brother's wife had gone into extended deep depression. Gorer himself was perplexed by his inability to cope with his feelings. He began to question others who had suffered similar losses.

What happened in the death of a child, a brother or sister, a parent, a spouse? The common denominator in most cases he examined was denial and inability to grieve. After extensive data collecting and weighing, Gorer concluded: "The majority of British people are today without adequate guidance as to how to treat death and bereavement and without social help in living through and coming to terms with the grief and mourning which are inevitable responses in human beings to the death of someone whom they loved." [3]

Similar conclusions about the American way of death have been reached in studies of grief reaction in this country.[4] Robert Fulton, introducing a compendium on *Death and Identity*, writes: "In America today we have come to a point in our history when we are beginning to react to death as we would to a communicable disease . . . . Those who are caught in the throes of death are isolated from their fellow human beings, while those who have succumbed to it are hidden quickly from view . . . . Death, like a noxious disease, has become a taboo subject, and as such it is both the object of much disguise and denial as well as of raucous and macabre humor." [5]

Unless it happens suddenly, as it did with Carole, dying can be a lonely, drawn-out process. No one has described the trauma of terminal illness with greater sensitivity than Elisabeth Kübler-Ross in her illuminating book *On Death and Dying*.[6] She discovered in her extensive counseling with dying patients that terminally ill persons most dread isolation, being left alone. We are so afraid of death that we have to resist running in the opposite direction when it strikes, especially in the inner circle of our family. Under such circumstances, we often are unable to do more than turn the doomed person over to the care of professionals.

Dr. Kübler-Ross has reported a study in which the time required for nurses to answer patients' lights was measured. "And they discovered that patients who were beyond medical help—terminally ill patients—had to wait twice as long as the others." [7] This, she argued, did not indicate the medical staff's callousness but a combination of our human dread of death and the primary commitment of medical science to the restoration of health, not to care of the dying.

Dread of death is not unique to twentieth-century man. There is more than beautiful poetry in the psalmist's timeless words: "Yea, though I walk though the valley of the shadow of death, I will fear no evil" (Ps. 23:4, KJV). The poet had experienced fear of death, else he would have had no reason to say that he was not afraid. Without the universal dread it is doubtful that another gem of scriptural assurance would have a place in the treasury of faith: "A thousand may fall at your side,/ten thousand at your right hand;/ but it will not come near you" (Ps. 91:7). We would like to take that literally, but, of course, the psalmist was expressing his faith in metaphor, because it does come near us, every one of us.

Several times in my life death has come close to me. How can I act as if nothing unusual has happened? What can I make of such experiences—since avoiding them was not an option? The question cannot be let alone because death does not leave us alone. Why are we afraid? Why do people appear embarrassed and thrown off stride when, after they have asked me what I am writing, I tell them it is about death? Why does my throat tighten when I tell them?

Ernest Becker, a brilliant teacher who died of cancer, wrote in his fine book *The Denial of Death* that "the idea of death, the fear of it, haunts the human animal like nothing else." [8] He is right. Man fears death because he values life so highly. People who talk lightly about death are usually those who have not been close to it. Logical argument about the necessity of death comes easily as long as it is the death of someone else or his loved one. Contemplation of our own death, or reflection upon the death of a person like Carole was to me, is quite another thing.

Our generation's dread of death is not new, but our denial of it while living in history's potentially most lethal time is proba-

bly singular. Two interrelated phenomena influence our attitude. One is secularization which is dedicated to making physical existence as pleasurable and painless as possible, and the
other is abandonment of religious faith, especially belief in life
after death.

Secularism is so pervasive that we cannot get enough distance
to comprehend how totally it affects us. We understand ourselves, quite unconsciously, as creatures of the secular age. Life
expectancy has been dramatically lengthened. Severe physical
discomfort has been eliminated for most of us. We take for
granted the enjoyment of a relatively mean temperature year
around. We have great mobility. Supermarkets dazzle the eye
with a variety and abundance of staple and exotic food.
Inexpensive clothing makes it unnecessary to worry about being
warm, only about being fashionable. There is a pill for every
contingency—for going to sleep or waking up, for nervousness
or depression, for high blood pressure or diabetes, or for the fear
of pregnancy. Whatever the problem, it can be handled—
almost.

Preoccupation with enjoyment of physical comfort has produced greater dedication to pleasure and peace of mind. That is
why the amusement and leisure industry is such a big business.
The unpardonable sin is to be sad. Unless one is vivacious,
bouncy, and smiling, one is not fully alive and, in certain religious circles, not fully dedicated to God.

One evening our first grandchild, then seven, while visiting
with her parents at our house, seemed preoccupied at dinner.
We scolded her for not eating, and I asked her if she were feeling
bad. She excused herself from the table and came back a few
minutes later with little notes on pink paper neatly wrapped for
each of her parents and grandparents. All the notes had the
same poignant apology written in her childish scrawl: "I am

sorry I've been so sad. Love, Carole." You see, the adult world to which she has to conform does not like sadness. To her we seemed to equate sadness with badness. At age seven, she had already learned an important lesson about our secular society.

Thoughts of death make us sad, and sadness is a negative emotion, an embarrassing invasion of our carefully orchestrated bliss. We are entitled to be happy—a much-abused term debased to mean a state of pain-free pleasure and of having one's desires fully and immediately gratified. Any somber or painful experience is an intrusion into Camelot.

The second aspect of this culture's death-denial is its widespread abandonment of the support and comfort of religious faith, especially belief in life after death. Gorer concluded that "this lack of accepted ritual and guidance is accompanied by a very considerable amount of maladaptive behaviour, from the triviality of meaningless 'busy-ness' . . . to the apathy of despair." [9] By pretending that death is incidental, marginal, and minimally disruptive, our culture has succeeded not in avoiding the dread but in heightening anxiety and deepening depression, producing widespread pathological reactions. Rejecting our father's belief structures, we have failed to develop any of our own.

The mushroom cloud hangs like a heavy pall over all our cities. Every schoolchild knows that we have enough missiles, and "the other side" has enough, to kill everybody on the planet two or three times. The reassurance that "a thousand may fall at your side, . . . but it will not come near you" will require some interpretation if missiles start firing. Ten thousand lost in this catastrophe, a hundred thousand wiped out in that air raid—it is almost as if we are not counting persons anymore, but megaunits of protoplasm. Human life is cheap, as the televison news and most of its shows remind us daily.

Further, as survival grows more perilous, knowledge of the universe keeps expanding. As the weapons become more deadly and the possibility of extinction more realistic, the size of the cosmos makes man appear by contrast to be less and less important. To multitudes the biblical doctrine of the supreme value of the individual and his eternal existence in a personal state is part of the lost bliss of childhood.

Here is a culture so confused about the meaning of death that it lionizes and enriches a stunt man for risking his life on a motorcycle by jumping over buses, while on the other hand it makes a national issue out of whether a girl lying for years in a coma like a vegetable should be artificially kept alive. In our excessive preoccupation with risk taking, we are like moths circling a flame in a lethal flirtation. Paradoxically, this is the generation which protects itself, shields itself, pampers itself, swallows pills of every description to ward off danger to itself, and battles endlessly against admitting the encroachment of age. Unable to talk about death or wrestle with the ageless questions of the meaning of life, we engage in a constant dance with a hooded partner whose presence we deny. This frantic embracing-rejecting behavior reflects loss of confidence in the biblical reassurances of the value of life to God.

The knowledge of death is deep within us. From the moment of birth we are dying. Even as the body reaches the apogee of its vitality, disintegration is going on. In our unconscious mind we know that we must die. My grandson at three years of age held a serious discussion with his mother about dying. He did not understand much about it, but he did not want to die or his parents to die. At three he already sensed the universal sadness. Whenever we become aware that we are dying, and as often as we are aware of it, we make a crucial decison whether to become morbidly preoccupied with the realization, neurotically shove it out of sight, or accept the reality and try to make sense of it. Whoever interprets the meaning of his existence through Christian faith will reject either of the first two options. Christians do not deny the pain of death but its finality.

That there are people without faith in the Christian promise of life eternal who, nonetheless, are neither morbidly preoccupied nor neurotically afraid, cannot be denied. Death means the dissolution of their existence. They seem satisfied to have it so, content to say that life's purpose is achieved when they have contributed something to the general welfare, bringing whatever hope they have for the race an infinitesimal fraction nearer fulfillment. I respect people who live with dignity, tranquillity, and meaning in such a frame. In effect, they are saying, "Why should I aspire to a separate and conscious personal existence after death? Once is enough. Indeed, should one not look forward to release from the struggle of being and welcome freedom from the prison of self?" Swinburne, champion of the stiff-upper-lip posture toward death, wrote that he thanked "With brief thanksgiving/Whatever gods that be,/That no life lives forever;/That dead men rise up never;/That even the weariest river/Winds somewhere safe to sea." [10]

To dismiss this view as sheer bravado is to refuse to hear another with the same respect we claim for our own witness. The words suggest more than "whistling in the dark." They more likely reflect denial of ultimate value to individual existence. But is life so painful and/or so trivial? Shall I renounce the hope of eternal life because I cannot believe that the life I now have is truly significant?

Suppose the Christian claim turns out to be right and resurrection cancels death's finality, with new and eternal life emerging from the experience of dying. That is what the New Testament testifies, and if it is to be trusted there is about us an indestructible and essential entity—a real, intelligible, identifiable person as much alive after death as before. If so, whether it pleases us or not, we have ourselves forever on hands. Dying will not deliver us from the necessity to deal with ourselves.

A noble and unselfish variation of the theme of "death is the end" is the notion of an "earthly immortality." This says: We do not live on after death except through those who come after us. We shall live in the memories of those who knew us and in the good works we left behind. Let us leave the camp of this earth a little neater and better provisioned for the next travelers than it was left for us.

Who can quarrel with such selfless sentiments? They magnify the perpetuation of the race, minimizing the survival of the individual. Further, they reflect the best of our sense of social responsibility, for we are indeed pilgrims blessed with others' beneficence and thus made responsible to be benefactors of still others. George Eliot nobly expressed this view in her beautiful verse:

> O may I join the choir invisible
> Of those immortal dead who live again
> In minds made better by their presence: live
> In pulses stirred to generosity,
> In deeds of daring rectitude: in scorn
> For miserable aims that end with self . . .
>
> So shall I join the choir invisible
> Whose music is the gladness of the world.[11]

That is beautiful poetry but bad Christian theology. To begin with, what shall we say to those who never got to live long enough or well enough to qualify for the choir? What will Eliot do with such persons, or is her choir an elite angelic host that welcomes Socrates but excludes John Clod? What about children who did not live much of their earthly lives at all? Are they candidates for this choir of human recollection that lives on in someone's memory because they left something to be remembered? And what about Carole, whose potential for singing the music of the spheres was just beginning to be realized?

A more serious problem with the notion of earthly immortality is the question: What happens ultimately? How shall we visualize the end? Suppose this process of succeeding generations passing through the camp, using the provisions left by predecessors, afterwards replenishing and enriching them, making the camp more comfortable, interesting, and perhaps less dangerous, goes on and on as far into the future as the mind can stretch. Visualize its continuation another ten thousand or hundred thousand years, each succeeding generation finding things better than the last and leaving them better than they found them. (This romantic and optimistic scenario of human evolution toward the ultimate emergence of a perfect race is contrary to the Bible, which understands all persons in each generation to be sinners needing redemption. Moreover, history does not encourage us to believe in human perfectability. What we see is man becoming more powerful, but not less selfish and exploitative.)

But to maintain the "campsite" metaphor to its logical end, there would finally arrive the last, most favored, most highly developed company of travelers. By their time the camp would be a veritable paradise, but they too, alas, would leave it just as their predecessors had left it. Only with their leaving, there would be no one else to come. No use to stock the camp with more elaborate and exotic provisions, for now the camp would stand deserted, like a ghost town in a gold-mining area. Mankind would have finally reached its corporate end—nothing— and its destination—nowhere. No one would remain to reflect upon man's achievements, to enjoy them or grieve over them, or to aspire to make them even more impressive. Maybe I do not understand, but the doctrine of an earthly immortality appears to have no other possible conclusion.

Thoughts of the ultimate cluster about one of three classic solutions to the mystery of life. The one just described suggests that existence as we know it finally winds down to a grinding halt. The thought that life—at least human life—will someday come to a total stop is not unthinkable. Man already has power in his arsenal sufficient to end physical existence. That life itself in the universe will cease to be is unimaginable.

Secondly, one may embrace one of the forms of the doctrine of reincarnation, a belief which antedates the Christian doctrine of resurrection by centuries. Its appeal is clear: The hope of another opportunity to live as yourself, although in another body and by another name and in another era, that you might improve on your past performance. Does one not always believe that one can do it better next time?

I would not suggest that either of these two ways of dealing with the continuity of life is without merit. I can say that as a Christian neither speaks to me because my confidence about personal survival and the redemption of the race lies in my belief in the resurrection of Christ. Earthly "links-on-the-chain-of-being" immortality leaves unanswered too many important questions such as, "Where shall the human race perpetuate itself after it has exhausted the resources and energy of this planet?" Most of all, it leaves unanswered the value of individual life. Did those who appeared earlier in the chain have no permanent meaning? Is their significance only that they kept the ember of life glowing for an infinitesimal moment in time? Or do they have an existence which is unique, individual, personal, and eternal? Christians affirm that they do and take seriously the promise of Jesus: "Because I live, you will live also" (John 14:19). To Job's ageless question "If a man die, shall he live again?" (14:14) the Christian, looking at Christ's empty tomb, says "Yes." And that is the third classic solution to the mystery of life.

I do not remember ever talking to Carole about death. She heard me preach about it, but that is not the same thing. We lived with the awareness of it in our family, with the death of a child and periodic deaths in the church family. I am unaware of any foreboding or premonition Carole might have had of her own death. I do not believe much in such forewarnings, not for myself at least, although I am quite willing for others to believe as they wish.

Yet I am sure Carole had thoughts about death simply because it was characteristic of her to embrace life, and death is inseparable from life. To reject contemplation of death is to ask that life be other than it is. However, that is a different mood from a brooding melancholy. She must have contemplated death, and her life was doubtless richer thereby. Among her papers I found the following poem:

> "Grandpa," the boy cried, "Come see this ugly sky
> And how that hawk is circling around our house
> Like death itself was creeping through the cellar door.
> What does it mean, why ain't it windin', and the sheep
> A-bleatin' on the hill?"
>
> The old man searched the noonday sky with weary eyes
> That knew without their seeing
> What the boy had seen.
> He knew the mighty quietness of gray that waited
> Like a mountain lion for his prey—
> He knew already how the rosy-tinted clouds
> Would mock him with the beauty of their strangeness—
> Mock the fear he had of them.

Yet Grandpa never really felt afraid whenever
They were overhead,
Because he knew that he was safe here in the valley
Down between the breasts of Mother Earth.

(And now the old man sits the boy down to tell him
Why his life is safe—to tell him a story, tell him
Not to think or worry when the sky is low or gray.)

"Hey, Boy, come back here to the porch and sit yourself,"
He said, "and listen while I talk about this valley
And the two hills where we keep our sheep.

"Time was when Indians roamed this valley—
Hunting, fishing, building altars to their goddess.
Many times the clouds would gather like today
But storms would never touch their campfires,
Never kill their game or children,
And they danced with heat the praise and thanks
Their painted bodies felt for being yet alive.

"So—many years swept by as dust does in the chicken yard,
And hunters ceased to wonder at or fear the sky.
They taught their children that no matter what
The other gods would do to punish all the tribe,
They should not be afraid, but trust their Mother Earth
Who held the valley like a child between her breasts
To keep it safe from harm.

"And, Boy, her hills have fed us and her valley
Kept us since the time when wagon trains first
'Whoaed' their sweating horses on this plain.
Just ask old Granny Whitby how it's been or
Doctor Kraus, or any man who herds his sheep on these two
    hills.

"We never bother when those men from Dallas
Call to warn of danger from the skies.
'Alarm, run, hide, there's fear in many hearts—'
We only laugh and trust our lives as we have always done.

"Now, Boy, out with you to the back and up to get the sheep.
The hill is high enough for you to see the valley
And the twin hill right across her.
You can watch the sky clear and the evening shadows
Slide across the earth to wrap us up in sleeping.
But don't be long because your Grandma will be serving."

The boy jumped off the porch and ran across the flat ground,
Rustlin' plain's grass with his levis.
He panted hard for his breath and for the lonely fear
Still in his stomach.
And he watched the angry face of clouds that hovered
Closer to the valley floor.

At last the hill was up ahead—the old familiar climb
Which led him to his sheep again and lifted him
Above the world of life into his world of dreams.
Quickly he climbed the hill, urged on by thoughts of some
Foreboding form which followed him in secret stealth.

He dared not look until amidst his sheep he grasped
Their warm wool in his hands and turned around—
And horror seized his hopes and twisted them like
The gray mass of whirling air which he saw poised o'er
The valley like the hawk over its prey.

Then suddenly as if to drown his uncontrolled screams
The demon fell upon the earth and from the hill
A wail arose as from a mother mourning for her child.

I have reproduced the lines in the form and order in which she
left them. The script appears to have been revised at several
places, and since I have discovered no other source, I conclude
that she composed the poem. Whoever wrote it knew the awesome Dread, the dark cloud. The hawk circles. Death creeps
through the cellar door. The boy saw it and, without the learned
inhibition of age, named the dread. The old man, without seeing, knew it was there, too. He had seen it many times before,

but children are not supposed to worry about such matters, so he told the boy a story of olden days, how their ancestors had always been spared. Though he had often watched the hawk as it circled and the dark cloud as it lowered, he had grown accustomed to them and would not permit himself to be afraid anymore.

The poem touches me deeply because it honestly puts the wonder that superimposes our pretending. On the back of the last page containing the poem about the boy and his grandpa were typed some poignant lines whose source I cannot find. They may have been Carole's:

> When in earth's bed we parallel each other,
> And whisper of the stillness that we feel,
> When we have scarred the soft breast of the Mother
> As does a fallen branch from yonder tree,
> Then will they heal us over with the soil
> And leave a sunken knot to prove life's toil.

Was Carole unduly preoccupied with thoughts of dying? Knowing her as well as I did, I am sure that she was not. She was intoxicated with life, enamored with the beauty and wonder of the world. But the point is that she did not neurotically ignore the important part of life which we experience as death. If what I have written in this book about Carole and death has any merit, it arises out of the conclusion that death is an awesome experience not to be treated academically, theoretically, sentimentally, or flippantly. But beyond that, I have found that the Christian understanding of death gives me a place to stand and strength to cope with my own moments of dying.

My life and hope are stirred by the Christian proclamation of the resurrection of Jesus Christ. His was a real death, as real as Carole's or anybody's; his burial a real burial that acknowledged the end of his human life, as burial does for every one of us. But the unshakable witness of the early church was that God raised Jesus from the dead. God cancelled the closing date of the drama of his life, and Jesus continued to live. God added a dimension to the death-burial routine, so that the occasion was not the end but a new beginning. "This Jesus God raised up, and of that we are all witnesses," one declared not many days after the event (Acts 2:32).

To palm off some lame explanation that the disciples sensed his spirit among them after his death or that they felt his continuing influence but never intended to suggest a real resurrection is to do manifest violence to their reports in the New Testament. We may refuse to credit the story, but we should not demythologize it into something not meant to be taken quite seriously. We do not understand the resurrection. Jesus is reported by the Gospels to be both physical and nonphysical in his resurrection form. He asked for food and was given a piece of broiled fish to eat (Luke 24:41–43). He also appeared and disappeared as one not limited by a physical body (Luke 24:36,51).

Paul, who not only believed the resurrection but also held that without it we have no gospel (1 Cor. 15:14), carefully explained that the nature of the resurrected state is nonmaterial. "Flesh and blood cannot inherit the kingdom of God, nor does the perishable inherit the imperishable" (1 Cor. 15:50). But that is not to suggest that there is no connection between the person you are before death and the person you are after death. The analogy Paul used is the relationship between the seed sown and the plant which grows from it. The two obviously are not the same, yet there is a vital connection between what is sown and what grows up. The potential of the seed is realized only in its death and "resurrection." Jesus is quoted in John 12:24 as using the same analogy.

Growing older has brought me the peace of accepting mystery

without denying me the eagerness to know. For that blessing I am grateful. The witnesses to Christ's resurrection seem quite reliable. They had no cause to lie. After all, the resurrection took them quite by surprise. When they discovered that he was alive, the face of the whole world changed for them. And it has for me. I have experienced his aliveness, too, though obviously not in the same way the witnesses to his resurrection experienced him.

Christ's resurrection has other meanings than that we ourselves will survive death. Foremost in his followers' minds was that the resurrection was God's ultimate and decisive act to vindicate Jesus' claim that in himself God had done a new and final thing to redeem creation. "God was in Christ reconciling the world unto himself" (2 Cor. 5:19) became a watchword for the church. But as in the resurrection God had completed the work begun in the creation, so the resurrection gave assurance that creation included the redemption of man from death.

And that is what I believe. I believe that Carole is alive, not just in my memory, for that may die; not just in her influence, for the time will come when no one will remember the life connected with her name. But Carole is alive, the person she was being the person she is, made more beautiful and holy by her presence with God.

Does it matter, then, that she did not get to live out her days and fulfill the promise she showed? Yes, it matters. It matters to me more than I can tell. I cannot accept that it makes no difference—to us, to her, to others who love her, to the world. That is one of the problems I cannot resolve. For one whose fulfillment seemed only beginning there was much unfinished business. But I believe that Carole is alive and well. The faith I have found through the Bible is a life-affirming, not a death-denying, faith. I continue to work on my understanding of it, being compelled to do so by some of the things written in this book. Death is all too real, but life is also real, and life is God's last word.

A magnificent statement of the triumph of life over death through Christ's victory is found in 2 Timothy 1:10. Earlier versions read: "Our Saviour Jesus Christ . . . hath abolished death, and hath brought life and immortality to light through the gospel." The word "abolished" is a poor translation of the text, and James Moffatt provides a better one: "Our Saviour Jesus Christ . . . put down death . . . ." Death has not been abolished. Believe me, it is never far away. "The last enemy to be destroyed is death," wrote Paul (1 Cor. 15:26), and it is only destroyed for us when we overcome it in resurrection.

But death has been "put down." Christ put death in its proper place. He put it in perspective. No longer the terrible antagonist and final victor, death now is seen as the servant and gatekeeper between two regions of God's realm—life and immortality. By means of the gospel—the redemption work of Christ's incarnation, life, death, and resurrection—light has been shed upon the areas on either side of the gateway, so that we now see that they are related. They are two sides of the same reality—God's province in two parts—life and immortality. With the light of the gospel turned upon death it takes on its proper appearance— Christ put it in its place—and we see that life here and life beyond the gate interpenetrate. Not all of life is on this side of the gate; not all of immortality lies on the other side.

"We know that we have already crossed over from death to life because we love the brothers," wrote another of the New Testament Christians (1 John 3:24). Loving the brothers does not provide us passage from death to life; rather, such love is the evidence that we have left the realm of death where love of self prevails, and have entered the realm of life. Note, of course, that the writer of those words and the people to whom they were written were very much alive in this world. They had not "passed on," but they had "crossed over," which is to say that they were already participating in the life that lies on the other side of the gate called "Death."

The New Testament faith, then, is a life-affirming faith, first and foremost. Only in caricature may it be represented as doleful, depressing, and death-oriented. Life is God's first and best wish for man. He made him and "breathed into his nostrils the breath of life; and man became a living being" (Gen. 2:7). We are made for life. Jesus said, "I came that they may have life, and have it abundantly" (John 10:10). That is what I think about when I think of Carole. She is alive. We shall always miss her here. Separation was and is indescribably painful to those of us who love her. But I believe that she is as much alive now as at that tragic instant of impact on the icy highway.

In a little book called *What We Live By*, there is a touching story of Christians in the second and third centuries driven underground by a hostile Roman government to labor until death in the Numidian mines of North Africa. Branded on the brow with a red-hot iron, chained so that they could not stand quite upright, frequently an eye gouged out, they were forced to live out their days in the dark and dank stench and to anticipate slow death in the mines. Here and there on smooth rocks, pathetic messages scribbled in charcoal recorded their presence. Some prayed for sympathy or to be remembered; others recorded the suffering of separation from family. "But the most frequent inscription, reiterated, as it were, in a frenzy of hope, was . . . *Vita, Vita, Vita* in long black lines, (which) seemed like a flight of swallows chasing one another toward the light which the poor scribbler knew was shining up above."[12] That is the essence of Christian faith. That is what this witness to Carole has been about—life.

Epilogue (Sermon on Death)

This sermon was first preached at the First Baptist Church, Danville, Virginia. On December 30, 1962, nine days after Carole's death, I read the sermon to the congregation of my second church, First Baptist, Greenville, South Carolina, with this explanation:

"Among our communications this week is a letter from a man I hardly know. He wrote: 'Many years ago I asked you to let me have a copy of a sermon I heard you deliver on death. I have kept this through the years, read and reread it and now I return it, enabled by my belief in God to know that the man who wrote it is now sustained by a power greater than himself who will come to comfort you and bind up the wounds of the broken hearted.' I, myself, have read and reread that old sermon this week, and I think I would like to share it with you."

The sermon has been reprinted numerous times since. It seems to bring comfort to bereaved persons and is reproduced here as a tribute to Carole.

Sorrow from the death of someone we love is like fire on crude ore—it burns with a terrible, devouring flame, but it proves what is there. Such sorrow brings out either our pitiful poverty of spirit or our deep resources.

More than any other experience, death is sobering and moving. In its presence the sophisticated covering of reserve we usually keep pulled tightly down over our raw feelings is often

137

ripped away, and the soul is bared. The reserve we count on to keep us from appearing too pious or sentimental or serious is swept away in such moments. Whoever stands close beside someone to whom death has become a poignant reality has the rare and awesome privilege of seeing people as they really are inside, with the bars down and the controls off. Then come forth unstudied words of praise for the loved and lost. Then pour out, often like a torrent, the cries of honest grief and hurt perplexity. Then, as at no other time, the heart is open for the reassurances of God's love which all persons, when they are not playing a part for others to see, long for with all their soul.

Elton Trueblood in his book *The Common Ventures of Life* suggests two reasons why death is such a soul-rending experience that is difficult to adjust to. First, of all the ventures common to man death is the greatest. It is the leap into the dark; death takes us to a bourne from which no traveler returns with words of reassurance. We know and can know so very little of the chasm which we cross. It is so dreadfully, awfully final.

Second, death is universal. Not everyone experiences the blessedness of a happy and fulfilling marriage, and not everyone has the joy of seeing the light of heaven in the eyes of his own child. But everyone dies. It is the democratizer of our common existence, the great leveler of mankind. Science may prolong life, and it may ease the pain of death, but it cannot abolish it.

Yet it is so very difficult for us to accept the reality of death—not so much perhaps for ourselves as for those whom we love who slip into the unseen—that as we were born into the world so shall we leave it. One of the signs of maturity is the ability to accept death as necessary.

But there must be something more than the mere acceptance of death as an accomplished and unavoidable fact. It is not enough simply to recognize that whatever we prize most we hold by a slender thread which may at any moment be broken. That knowledge by itself could be the most brutal fatalism. There is much more. There are the yearnings, the unfulfilled hopes and ambitions, the love for life, which death as the final event would make a hollow mockery. There is the evidence of a sensible, orderly, designed universe which could not just have happened and which encourages us to reject the finality of death as not only undesirable but as unreasonable.

I do not underestimate the value of traditional and familiar arguments for the continuation of life beyond the event of death, but I must say that I do not believe in life after death because it is reasonable to believe. I believe in it because Christ was raised from the dead and encourages us to take heart from his resurrection. Because he lives, we shall live also. The simple intention of this sermon is to recall what Jesus said about the nature of the resurrected life and to look at his attitude towards death. Beside all of man's arguments for or against the reasonableness of life after death I set Jesus' claims. He is my authority. I shall take what he says most seriously.

His resurrection changes the face of reality for me. It breathes the breath of hope upon a dying world and causes me to cry with the apostle Paul, "O death, where is thy sting? O death, where is thy victory? . . . Thanks be to God, who gives us the victory through our Lord Jesus Christ" (1 Cor. 15:55,57).

What is this unique contribution made by Jesus? How does Christ help when death comes? What does he know that the philosophers don't? Our answers are partial because our understanding is partial. We see through a glass darkly. Who can understand the mystery of the Lord? The issues are too vast and deep for the resources of man's mind. But we do know what our Lord said, and that helps.

Caring

One of the words that continually comes from the Gospels about Jesus is that he cared deeply for people. He not only cared for them but also liked them. He enjoyed children's laughter, the gaiety of marriages, and the warm fellowship of friends at meals. But he was also "a man of sorrows, and acquainted with grief" (Isa. 53:3). He knew how to laugh when it was appropriate and how to weep when that was appropriate.

He helped people in grief by genuinely caring for them. That sounds simple, but is by no means automatic. Jesus was never glib or casual or merely trivial or sentimental. Nothing is less comforting—though doubtless well-intentioned—than the Pollyanna, it-might-have-been-worse or everything-is-for-the-best, approach to someone's grief. Such minimizing by people who presume to comfort is of no help. "How then will you comfort me with empty nothings?" Job asked his friends in exasperation (21:34). Many a person too polite to say such a thing has endured in silence the casual imposition of others doing their duty towards the bereaved but not really caring enough to be sensitive.

One of the occasions where Jesus wept was standing with his friends, Mary and Martha, and sharing their grief over the death of their brother, Lazarus. How could anyone ever be guilty of casualness in the presence of death after reading John 11? He was so sensitive, so caring, as he shared their sorrow.

But that was not unusual. He was often present to the unbearable strain felt by others. Once a foreign woman, a Syrophoenician, whose daughter was critically ill, entreated him for his help. The exchange between them as he restored her daughter to health is one of the most touching scenes in the Gospels. She had been at the end of her resources, but he had intervened and saved the child. And there was the Jewish ruler,

Jairus, whose little daughter was dead when Jesus arrived. "Fear not," he assured the grief-stricken father, "only believe." And remember that among the many whom he helped in their distress was a dying thief whose cry of penitence Jesus heard and responded to even though he himself was enduring the agony of dying on the cross.

The night before his death, so John reports, he was sitting in the upper room concerned about others, as usual, more than about himself. "I am going away," he began to tell them, "but I will not leave you as desolate orphans. I will come to you. For the Father will send another Comforter like myself to be with you forever, whom the world cannot lay hands upon and kill because he is spirit and will be with you and within you" (see John 14).

Thus, when sorrow comes and we gather to read together the majestic words of John 14, we know that he is with us yet, speaking the strong words of comfort and understanding: "Let not your hearts be troubled; believe in God, believe also in me" (v. 1).

I take heart in the fact that he did not give us simple, shallow answers to the problem of dying. I am grateful that he did not leave us some shabby sentiment as his contribution to our effort to accept it. I am comforted by knowing that his capacity to care was infinitely greater than mine and that he must have therefore measured the depths of the ocean of sorrow while I have only waded in the surf. It helps me to believe that he knows and really cares.

Understanding

But he brings us more than sympathy for our hours of grief. His gifts include insight and understanding into the meaning of life and the reason for hope that it continues beyond death.

Nowhere is his view of the nature of life as eternal, unlimited by the boundaries of time and space, more clearly expressed than in a conversation with a group of Sadducees who, as Matthew reports it, approached him with a question about life after death.

The Sadducees were a prominent religious party who controlled the Temple and the services of religion. While the Pharisees espoused belief in the resurrection of the dead, the Sadducees denied that it was possible and argued that Scripture (our Old Testament) did not teach it.

The example they put forward as a test case was probably an old familiar story designed to show how absurd was any belief that life went on beyond the grave. The story constituted a "Which-came-first-the-chicken-or-the-egg?" proposition. It was meant to be unanswerable and thus meant to reduce the entire argument to absurdity.

According to the story, a woman's husband died childless and, in accordance with the law of Moses, her dead husband's brother married her so that the deceased man might have an heir. Unfortunately, the second husband also died leaving a childless widow, so the third brother married her. He, too, died without offspring, and this went on through the course of the woman's marriage to seven brothers, all of whom preceded her in death. At last, she died. Then came the "clincher." "In the resurrection whose wife will she be since all seven had been married to her?" the Sadducees asked with a knowing smile.

In Jesus' answer lies such depth that one wonders why it has been so often overlooked in our consideration of the Christian understanding of life after death. They were wrong on two counts, he said. They who presumed to understand and be devoted to Scripture did not really know it; nor did they know the power of God. Neither did the Scripture rule out the hope of resurrection; nor was the power of God limited by the power of death over our human frame. Here are two pivotal insights into the problem.

First, "In the resurrection they neither marry nor are given in marriage, but are like angels in heaven." This is to say, the physical ties are all severed at death. Here in this life we are all tied up in a bundle of physical relationships: husband and wife, child and parent, brother and sister, friend and friend. But at death the physical ties fall away. The body with which we have identified the person we love, ceases to be and returns to the earth in decay.

They "are like angels in heaven." This I take to mean that at death all that is physical ceases to exist and we become spirit. We are freed from the bonds of time and space. The body which we pamper and pet and doctor and dress up is only a temporary home for the person who goes on living when the body has become useless and is discarded.

Paul can help us perhaps a little further at this point. He was a tentmaker by profession. Thus once, in describing eternal life with God, he compared death to the taking down of a tent when you got ready to move on. Tents are for temporary habitation; they are not permanent residences. So he said: "We know that if the earthly tent we live in is destroyed [and it surely will be], we have a building from God, a house not made with hands, eternal in the heavens" (2 Cor. 5:1). This is in keeping with the insight of Jesus. At death the body becomes less important because the person living there has moved out.

Jesus' second clue to the nature of life beyond the chasm of death complements the first. It is the reverse side, like the heads and tails of a coin. The two do not contradict one another but belong to each other and one is incomplete without the other. "And as for the resurrection of the dead, "Jesus added, "have you not read what was said to you by God, 'I am the God of

Abraham, and the God of Isaac, and the God of Jacob?' He is not God of the dead, but of the living" (Matt. 22:31–32).

"He is God of the living," Jesus claimed. Hear his implication: Do not jump to the conclusion that since man becomes spirit at death, and that which is mortal in him decays, therefore life after death is an airy, nonpersonal existence. Jesus did not believe in a return of the human spirit to be joined with the Universal Spirit, the human spark struck from the wheel of God being reunited with the Wheel. He did not believe in Nirvana and the loss of individuality, the mind becoming an infinitesimal part of the Divine Mind. We might prefer to have it that way. To have oneself forever on one's hands might be an awesome prospect. Yet that is precisely what the words of Jesus suggest. God is the God of living people—Abraham, Isaac, and Jacob, though physically dead hundreds and hundreds of years when Jesus spoke the words, were still Abraham, Isaac, and Jacob. God is God of living persons. Persons are indestructible. You are indestructibly you, and I am I.

Here are two critical insights into what we may think of life after death. Think of it, said Jesus, as both spiritual and personal. "We know that flesh and blood cannot inherit the kingdom of God," wrote Paul to the Corinthians. He had no crude notion of the resuscitation of the dead body. But one should not conclude thereby that Paul doubted for a moment the reality of the resurrection and the continuance of a personal life beyond the grave.

Much beyond these two clues Jesus did not go. Why he did not tell us more is part of the mystery. Perhaps it is true, as some have suggested, that the nature of life in the next stage of our existence is so radically different from what we are accustomed to that there are no categories of thought, no descriptive words which can give any true picture to our minds. How can one make a blind man "see" the glorious beauty of a sunset, or a stone-deaf man "hear" the moving tones of a great symphony? Or how can a beautiful butterfly stoop to explain his new life to a struggling, earthbound caterpillar? Perhaps our earthly understanding is too limited to take in much of the glory of the things which are to come and we should be content to say with Paul, "Eye has not seen, nor ear heard, neither have entered into the heart of man, the things which God has prepared for them that love him."

We believe that he gave us enough, all we need, and perhaps all we could understand, of the essentially nonphysical nature of life after death, while reassuring us of its essentially personal nature. If we believe what he said we trust that we shall always hold a direct, recognizable relationship with the persons we now are.

Trusting

Beyond his caring and the understanding he has shared with us, Jesus has done one other thing. He asks us to trust him and our heavenly Father as we deal with death. Where we cannot understand he bids us believe. What a terrifying world it would be if we could trust no one, depend upon no one's veracity and motive. Jesus asks us to believe in the trustworthiness of the Father. "If you then, who are evil, know how to give good gifts to your children, how much more will your Father who is in heaven give good things to those who ask him!" (Matt. 7:11). If human fathers may be trusted, how much more the heavenly Father!

Jesus' own example of trust encourages us. In the garden of Gethsemane he asked that he might be spared the suffering of the cross and death, but he concluded that prayer with an expression of complete confidence in the purpose and goodness of God: "Nevertheless, not as I will, but as thou wilt" (Matt. 26:39). And as he hung dying upon the cross he reaffirmed that confidence when he said, "Father, into Thy hands I commit my spirit."

James Gordon Gilkey has related in a sermon a touching story about a nineteenth-century Congregational minister of New England, named John Todd. Left an orphan when he was six, John Todd had been reared by an aunt who had seen him through Yale and divinity school. During Todd's pastorate in Pittsfield, Massachusetts, he received a pitiful letter from his aged aunt, telling him in great distress that her doctor had told her that she was the victim of an incurable disease and that death was not only inevitable but imminent. He had been to college and seminary; he had read books and was wise. Could he tell her about death? Was there anything to fear?

This was John Todd's answer: "It is now thirty-five years since I, a little boy of six, was left quite alone in the world. You sent me word you would give me a home and be a kind mother to me. I have never forgotten the day when I made the long journey of ten miles from my home in Killingworth to your home in North Killingworth. I can still recall my disappointment when I learned that instead of coming for me yourself you had sent your colored man Caesar to fetch me. I can still remember my tears and anxiety as, perched on your horse and clinging tight to Caesar, I started for my new home."

Then Todd went on to describe his childish anxiety as darkness fell before the journey was ended and how he wondered if his aunt would have gone to bed before he got there. Presently, he wrote, they had ridden out of the woods into a clearing and, sure enough, there was a friendly candle in the window, and his aunt was waiting at the door. He remembered her warm arms around him, lifting him gently—a tired and bewildered little boy—down from the horse. She had given him supper beside the bright fire in her hearth and then had taken him to his room and sat beside him till he dropped off to sleep.

"You are probably wondering why I am now recalling all these things to your mind," he added. "Some day soon God will send for you, to take you to a new home. Don't fear the summons, the strange journey, the messenger of death. At the end of the road you will find love and a welcome; you will be safe in God's care and keeping. God can be trusted—trusted to be as kind to you as you were to me so many years ago." [1]

God can be trusted! In the last analysis, Christians have no more persuasive word. God can be trusted. That does not resolve all the mysteries or answer all the questions, but it gives us enough to build our lives around. God is trustworthy. He is Lord of life and death, and he is to be trusted. "Let not your hearts be troubled," Jesus said, "believe!"

Notes

CHAPTER 1

1. Emily Dickinson, J. 1078. (Numbering of poems established by Thomas Johnson.)
2. Lord Gordon, George Byron, "Childe Harold's Pilgrimage."
3. Alfred Tennyson, "In Memoriam: A. H. H."

CHAPTER 3

1. Kahlil Gibran, *The Prophet* (New York: Alfred A. Knopf, 1923), p. 66.

CHAPTER 6

1. Stewart Alsop, *Stay of Execution* (Philadelphia: J. B. Lippincott Co., 1973), p. 68.
2. David K. Switzer, *The Dynamics of Grief* (Nashville: Abingdon Press, 1970).
3. Edgar N. Jackson, "Grief," *Concerning Death: a Practical Guide for the Living*, ed. Earl A. Grollman (Boston: Beacon Press, 1974), p. 3.
4. Robert E. Kavanaugh, *Facing Death* (Los Angeles: Nash Publishing Co., 1972), p. 107.

5. Colin Murray Parkes, *Bereavement: Studies of Grief in Adult Life* (London: Tavistock Publishers, Ltd., 1972), p. 39.

6. Ibid.

7. Elisabeth Kübler-Ross, "What Is It Like to Be Dying?" *American Journal of Nursing* 71, no. 1 (January 1971): 58.

8. Richard B. Sewall, *Williams College Alumni Review* (Fall 1975), p. 4.

9. Elisabeth Kübler-Ross, *Death: the Final Stage of Growth* (Englewood Cliffs: Prentice-Hall, Inc., 1975), p. ix.

10. Thornton Wilder, *Our Town*.

11. Albert L. Blackwell, "Schleiermacher's Sermon at Nathanael's Grave," *The Journal of Religion* 57, no. 1 (January 1977), p. 75.

CHAPTER 7

1. As quoted by John Hick, *Evil and the God of Love* (London: Collins, The Fontana Library Edition, 1975), p. 5.

2. Mary Baker Eddy, *Science and Health with Key to the Scriptures.* Published by the trustees under the will of Mary Baker G. Eddy (Boston, 1934), pp. 107–164.

3. L. D. Johnson, *Out of the Whirlwind: the Major Message of Job* (Nashville: Broadman Press, 1971).

4. P. T. Forsyth, *The Justification of God* (London: Latimer House Ltd., 1917).

5. Ibid, p. 211.

6. Ibid, pp. 220–221.

7. Hick, p. 5.

8. Blackwell, p. 74.

CHAPTER 8

1. John Luckey McCreery, "There Is No Death," *Masterpieces of Religious Verse*, ed. James Dalton Morrison (New York: Harper and Brothers, 1948), p. 585.

2. Geoffrey Gorer, *Death, Grief, and Mourning* (Garden City, New York: Doubleday, Inc., 1965), p. 114.

3. Ibid., p. 110.

4. Cf. Earl A. Grollman, ed., *Concerning Death: a Practical Guide for the Living* (Boston: Beacon Press, 1974), pp. x–xvii.

5. Robert Fulton, ed., *Death and Identity* (New York: John Wiley and Sons, Inc., 1964), p. 4.

6. Elisabeth Kübler-Ross, *On Death and Dying* (New York: Macmillan Co., 1969).

7. Ibid., quoted from *The American Journal of Nursing* 71, no. 1 (January 1971): 57.

8. Ernest Becker, *The Denial of Death* (New York: Free Press, 1976), p. 5.

9. Gorer, p. 110.

10. Algernon Charles Swinburne, "The Garden of Proserpine:"

11. George Eliot, "O May I Join the Choir Invisible."

12. Ernest Dimnet, *What We Live By* (New York: Simon and Schuster, 1932), p. 302.

EPILOGUE

1. James Gordon Gilkey, "Christianity's Message to the Modern World," *The American Pulpit Series* 6 (New York: Abingdon-Cokesbury Press, 1945), pp. 50–53.

A Tribute to L. D. Johnson

Remarks by Francis W. Bonner
at the meeting of the Board of Trustees
on October 11, 1994, honoring L. D. Johnson

L. D. Johnson died on December 20, 1981, at the age of sixty-five. The loss went far beyond the Furman campus to the thousands of people he inspired through his preaching, writing, and spiritual leadership.

Born on a farm in Walters, Oklahoma, Johnson lost both parents when he was only three and was reared, with his two brothers, by grandparents. Johnson, who once said he had never considered any career but ministry, prepared for that vocation first at George Washington University and then at The Southern Baptist Theological Seminary, from which he obtained both Master of Theology and Doctor of Theology degrees.

While he was a sophomore at George Washington University, L. D. met and fell in love with a pretty senior who was a secretary in the Commerce Clearing House. L. D. was working as an elevator operator. He and Marion Ervin were married in 1937, and she continued to work to provide support and encouragement as L. D. finished college and earned advanced degrees at the seminary. They had four children, and she continued to help in numerous ways. For example, she planned all their trips, tours, and vacations. Edna Hartness, the Johns, and the Bonners were among those whom L. D. conducted on an extended tour of the Holy Land and parts of Europe. After L. D. took the position at Furman, Marion was for sixteen years on the staff of the University library. Surely, L. D.'s effectiveness as minister, preacher, chaplain, and author owed much to the kind of love and support Marion provided.

L. D.'s ministry was divided almost equally between church and college. he was pastor of First Baptist Church of Danville, Virginia, from 1943 to 1959, and then for three years was chairman of the religion department at the University of Richmond. In 1962 he became pastor of the First Baptist Church of Greenville, [South Carolina], and in 1967 chaplain and professor of religion at Furman.

For many years, up until his final hospitalization, Dr. Johnson wrote a weekly newspaper column that appeared in the *Greenville News* and *Greenville Piedmont* and other newspapers. A selection of his columns, *Moments of Reflection*, was published in 1980.

He also wrote *An Introduction to the Bible, Out of the Whirlwind, Israel's Wisdom, The Morning after Death*, and a study of Proverbs, Ecclesiastes, and the Song of Solomon.

He was widely sought after as [a] preacher and lecturer. In 1979 he was the opening speaker at the first National Congress on Church-Related Colleges and Universities, an ecumenical conference held at Notre Dame. He spoke at Carson-Newman College, Mercer University, and Averett College. He delivered a series of lectures to the Christian Life Commission of the Southern Baptist Convention in March 1981.

Dr. Johnson received the George Washington Medal of Honor for a newspaper column in 1964 and in 1978 was named William R. Kenan, Jr., professor of religion at Furman University. Under his guidance, the Furman Pastors School became the largest program of continuing theological education in the nation.

The quality of L. D.'s preaching never waned. It simply got better. He had a genius for the arresting phrase, for clarity, and for the logical development of a subject. He kept the attention of the listener from start to finish. He made one think along with him, and he left the listener amazed at his ability to make a profound idea simple, logical, and convincing. His writings were like that, too. His style has been compared with Willa Cather. What he said and wrote was so lucid, so seemingly simple, and yet so poignant that there seemed to be *no* style. How deceptive! Students of writing and speaking can find no better model.

As a pastor, L. D. was the man we all came to know—warm, compassionate, concerned, gentle, understanding. He loved people, and with each person it was an individual thing. A phrase heard about him frequently was "He was my friend." But during the mid-1960s, when race relations was a lively issue in greenville, L. D.'s forthright stance on racial justice annoyed a few of the pillars of the First Baptist Church.

Fearing that he might decide that he would be happier in another position and leave Greenville, he was invited to become Furman's chaplain, teach some classes as a professor of religion, preach and speak as much as he desired, and give full vent to his extraordinary abilities as a scholar and writer. He accepted the offer. On that day Fortune smiled on Furman—indeed!

As chaplain, L. D.'s path was not always smooth. During his early years at Furman we still had some rebels, students whose only cause was to attack the establishment—and for them he represented the religious segment of that authority. The student newspaper was vitriolic in its attacks, and this gentle, humble man was deeply hurt. Fortunately, most students and faculty perceived the injustice and reacted accordingly. Soon the students and all others at Furman began to appreciate L. D. for his true worth. he became a friend, counselor, confidant, and comforter to generation after generation of students.

He endured many personal tragedies, but the death of his daughter Carole wounded him most deeply. But his strength was such that on the following Sunday he preached one of his most powerful and poignant sermons. It was on death.

In 1976 he asked for a leave of absence to spend six weeks in England at the places where Carole had been in school. He wanted to write a book on death, and he wished to do it where that beautiful girl had spent so happy a time. He and Marion went, and the result was his moving and masterful volume, *The Morning after Death*.

L. D. stared death squarely in the face and defied that last enemy to do its worst, secure in a faith that foresaw no finality.

He left us a legacy rich and rare. He taught us that the love of God through His Son is more than a beautiful theory. It can be a redemptive reality—for that was the way L. D. lived. He was a great man—great from the pulpit and platform, great in conveying the truths of life through his remarkable writings, great in his brilliance as a scholar and teacher. But those who had the good fortune to know him will remember him best for his unpretentious compassion—his deep, calm, and genuine love for people.

I conclude these remarks with a bit of free verse, in which I attempt to express what L. D. meant to many of us.

Of Darkness and Light

"The people who walked in darkness have seen a great light."
(Isaiah 9:2; Matthew 4:16)

When L. D. Johnson died a light was gone,
Or so it seemed,
A light which had shined brilliantly and clear.
And darkness dense,
Seemingly impenetrable,
Enveloped us for whom the light had shined.
For he had helped us live in light,
Light of mind and spirit,
Light by which truth was seen and known,
Known in all its loveliness.
Would his leaving
Leave us then to live in darkness,
darkness dense and dismal
Stifling?

But he would say,
Would smile and say,
it must not be so.
The light by which you live
Was not mine to give;
It was there before
And must be there still.
Perhaps I helped to open eyes,
helped some to see the light which was there,
And is there.
If perchance I helped to open eyes,
Mine and yours,
I rejoice.

What better thing can we do,
You and I?
Let your eyes be open still
And never close.
If I have helped to make it so—
What more can any life have wished?

Yes, the light he helped us see
Still is there,
Made brighter, clearer by the legacy he left us,
The light by which we search for truth
And by which truth is known when seen.
We hope the way he helped us see
Will be the way
By which we thus can help
To open other eyes,
Those among us
Who are now searching, seeking hope,
Even now.

He would want it thus to be.

Francis W. Bonner
Vice President and Provost Emeritus
Furman University